The Weird and Wonderful Story of Gin

The Weird and Wonderful Story of Gin

From the Seventeenth Century to the Present Day

Angela Youngman

PEN & SWORD
HISTORY

AN IMPRINT OF PEN & SWORD BOOKS LTD.
YORKSHIRE – PHILADELPHIA

First published in Great Britain in 2022 by
Pen & Sword History
An imprint of
Pen & Sword Books Ltd
Yorkshire - Philadelphia

ISBN 978 1 39900 276 9

A CIP catalogue record for this book is available from the British Library.

Printed and bound in England
By CPI (UK) Ltd.

Pen & Sword Books Ltd incorporates the Imprints of Pen & Sword Archaeology,
Atlas, Aviation, Battleground, Discovery, Family History, History, Maritime,
Military, Naval, Politics, Railways, Select, Transport, True Crime, Fiction,
Frontline Books, Leo Cooper, Praetorian Press, Seaforth Publishing,
Wharncliffe and White Owl.

For a complete list of Pen & Sword titles please contact

PEN & SWORD BOOKS LIMITED
47 Church Street, Barnsley, South Yorkshire, S70 2AS, England
E-mail: enquiries@pen-and-sword.co.uk
Website: www.pen–and–sword.co.uk

or

PEN AND SWORD BOOKS
1950 Lawrence Rd, Havertown, PA 19083, USA
E-mail: uspen-and-sword@casematepublishers.com
Website: www.penandswordbooks.com

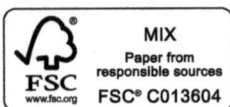

Contents

Chapter 1

How It All Began

Born in rebellion and revolt, via hedonism, crime, social upheaval and uncertainty, not counting a pandemic, gin has had an extremely chequered history. From a drink of the wealthy, to the comfort of the poorest of poor, from a boring uncool drink to a fashionable pleasure, the story of gin is one of continual transformation. And it all started with a simple drink, beloved of the Dutch.

The word gin derives from genever (the anglicised form of jenever). This is a botanically rich, clear, malted grain-based spirit, which can now only be made in the Netherlands or Belgium. Since 2008, an official AOC (*appellation d'origine contrôlée*) has been in place, denoting exactly what constitutes genever and stressing that it can only be produced in these two countries and very specific areas of France and Germany.

No one quite knows exactly where and when genever originated. According to legend, the story begins with a Dutch doctor and alchemist named Sylvius de Bouve working at the University of Leiden, who distilled medicines with juniper berry oil. The problem with this story is that it is known medicines containing the distilled berries of juniper were on sale in the Netherlands by the sixteenth century – and Sylvius de Bouve was born in the seventeenth century. During his tenure at the University of Leiden, he was undoubtedly distilling juniper for medicines, but none of his research papers contain any references to genever. In addition, he was not the first person to distil with juniper. There are written references to genever as long ago as the thirteenth century within *Der Naturen Bloeme* (The Flower of Nature) by Jacob van Maerlant, an adaptation of an earlier book *De Natura Rerum* (The Nature of Things) by Thomas of

Cantimpré. Much of the content of *De Nature Rerum* derives from classical Greek and Roman sources.

The invention of the still is believed to date back to Maria the Jewess, a first-century alchemist living in Alexandria. She is said to have been the first true distiller, inventing the bain marie, as well as the tribikos (a device with three arms allowing substances to be purified by distillation) and a kerotakis (a device to heat substances to collect vapours).

The Jenevermuseum in Hasselt, Belgium claims that genever was first produced in Flanders during the thirteenth century. At this period, Flanders was a geographical area covering several parts of the Low Countries including Holland, Luxemburg and parts of what is now northern France. Genever was initially distilled as a medicinal tonic but soon became popular as a social, relaxing drink. Precise dates and records as to when this happened are unknown, but distilleries in Flanders were certainly being taxed from the late fifteenth century onwards. *Jenever in de Lage Landen* (published by Stichting Kunstboek and the Jenevermuseum) contains references to many different recipes of 'brandewijn' (burnt wine) and jenever from the thirteenth century onwards, describing the production of brandewijn flavoured with different herbs and spices, especially juniper berry.

According to Tristan Stephenson's *The Curious Bartender's Gin Palace*, potentially one of the first references to a gin-based recipe occurred in the Duchy of Guelders. He wrote:

> In 1495, a wealthy merchant from a region known as the Duchy of Guelders (now part of the Netherlands, near Arnhem) decided it would be a good idea to have a book written for him. Being a household guide, the book documented some of the lavish recipes he and his family were enjoying at the time. Included was a brandy recipe made from '10 quarts of wine thinned with clear Hamburg beer'. After distillation, the

liquid would be redistilled with 'two handfuls of dried sage, 1lb of cloves, twelve whole nutmegs, cardamom, cinnamon, galangal, ginger, grains of paradise' and – crucially – 'juniper berries'. The spices were placed in a cloth sack and suspended above the distillate, allowing the vapours to extract their flavour. Grinding diamonds over white truffle is as close a comparison as I can imagine to expressing the extravagance of such a recipe during that period. It's for this reason that it's highly unlikely that the drink was intended for anything other than sinful pleasures.

Distillers Cooper King experimented with that recipe in 2017, using a medieval style beer recommended by Monnik Beer Company. After two experimental attempts at distillation, Cooper King bottled it at 94% proof commenting that 'the gin is delicious at this proof, with a lot of sharp edges smoothed off, and the botanicals shine brightly.'

A slightly different recipe was tried by the Gin 1495 project involving Philip Duff, Dave Wondrich, Dave Broom and Gaz Regan, completed in 2015. Their recipe was discovered in another 1495 cookbook from the East Netherlands, formerly owned by Sir Hans Sloane and now in the British Library. This recipe involved a blend of brandy and Marc/Pomace as well as nutmeg, ginger, galangal, seeds of paradise, cloves, cinnamon, cardamom, sage and juniper. One part botanicals to nine parts wine distillate were used in the recipe. Two versions of the resultant gin were created, one at 42% ABV, which had very bold flavours and was exceptionally dry with a touch of salty brine and menthol pepper notes. The second version was made using more juniper and citrus, together with the addition of angelica, creating a more citrus, spicy drink with an ABV of 45%.

A further recipe for jenever can be found in a manuscript dated 1552, *Een Constelijck Distileerboec*, written by Antwerp-based Philippus Hermanni. This booklet is particularly interesting because it contains the first printed recipe of what Hermanni describes as 'jeneverbessenwater' (juniper berry water). He was also the first writer to mention 'geest' (spirit) when referring to alcohol vapour. His booklet became the most important instructional manual for distillers from the sixteenth to the eighteenth century.

Genever was enjoyed by everyone, not just the nobility. While genever destined for the nobility and wealthy merchants was more likely to include expensive exotic herbs and spices, ordinary people concentrated on using spices abundantly available within the locality, such as juniper berry, caraway seeds, cardamom, aniseed and coriander. Sometimes genever was only grain alcohol or maltwine flavoured with a little juniper berry.

Taverns and alcohol drinking definitely became a central part of local culture within Holland and Flanders, with tavern scenes being depicted by Dutch artists such as Brueghel, Bosch, van de Velde, Jan Steen and Teniers. Pieter Brueghel the Younger's *Peasants Merrymaking Outside the Swan Inn in a Village Street (1630)* and Jan Steen's *Merrymaking in a Tavern with a Couple Dancing* (*c.* 1670), are typical of this genre.

Schiedam, just outside Rotterdam, has become one of the centres of genever production. Genever has been distilled at Schiedam for centuries, leading to a steady increase in distillery numbers from 37 to 250. By the late eighteenth century, there were nearly 400 roasters and distilleries in the area exporting genever worldwide.

How did genever get to England?

No one knows just when genever first appeared in England, but it seems to have been a gradual process.

It is likely that cross border links between monasteries led to an exchange of information, with monks distilling liquids for a variety of purposes. Certainly, by the late medieval period there were many Dutch wool merchants trading and living in England who imported genever and introduced the drink to their customers.

In parallel to what was going on in the Low Countries, from 1534 onwards there was a steady increase in the number of distilleries operating in England. The effects of the Reformation and Henry VIII's Dissolution of the Monasteries had resulted in hundreds of skilled monks entering civilian life. Many of these had served as alchemists and herbalists within their monasteries, and turned to distilling liquids as a way of earning a living.

Later in the sixteenth century, English soldiers and sailors fighting in the Low Countries during the reign of Elizabeth I encountered genever and brought it back with them to England. In 1623, Philip Massinger's play, *The Duke of Milan* contains references to drinking genever. During the 1630s, Dutch ships bearing supplies of genever were frequent visitors to ports like London, Bristol, Plymouth and Liverpool.

The seventeenth century was one of considerable strife throughout Europe, resulting in widespread conflicts involving soldiers of many nationalities, including the Dutch and English. Within the British Isles, the Parliamentarian success in the Civil War resulted in many Royalists going into exile in the Netherlands, inevitably becoming more acquainted with the local drink, genever. Although Charles II regained the throne in 1660, his successor, James, was eventually deposed due to disputes over policy and religion. James' Protestant daughter Mary and her husband, William of Orange, were invited to take the throne. It was a decision that marked a major milestone in the history of gin.

When William and Mary acceded the throne in 1689, distilling of spirits had already been taking place in England for some decades, albeit on a relatively small scale. Charles I had granted a Royal Charter to the Worshipful Company of Distillers in 1638, giving them a monopoly regarding the production of 'Aqua Vitae, Aqua Composita, and other strong and hot waters'. The founders of this Worshipful Company included influential people such as Queen Henrietta Maria's physician, Dr Thomas Cademan, and Sir Théodore Turquet de Mayerne, physician to James I and Charles I.

Medical practitioners were often involved in distilling due to their need to create alcohol for use in their medicines. Such strong waters had been prescribed to sufferers from a variety of ailments, including constipation, for many years. This was one of the key reasons given for creating the Worshipful Company of Distillers. The stated purpose of the Worshipful Company of Distillers was to supply 'those that be aged and weak in time of sudden qualms and pangs' in addition to supplying 'the King's ships and merchant ships for use shipboard and for sale to foreign nations'.

Among the recipes created by de Mayerne was one for a liquid involving rue, sage, lavender, marjoram, wormwood, rosemary, red roses, thistle, pimpernel, valerian, juniper berries, bay berries, angelica, cirrus bark, coriander, sandalwood, basil, grains of paradise, pepper, ginger, cinnamon, saffron, mace, nutmeg, cubeb, cardamom and galingale.

William of Orange's arrival heralded a dramatic change in the fortunes of genever in the British Isles. Although versions of juniper-based drinks had been common for medicinal purposes, genever (also known as Hollands) had been an imported drink and invariably more expensive. From 1689, this situation began to alter. William was very fond of genever and increasing numbers of people began drinking it in his honour and to signify their support for the new regime. Dutch records indicate that demand became so great that distillers were loading ships with genever immediately after it was produced, rather than letting it rest for a few weeks as had previously been the practice.

One of William's first legislative actions was to declare war on France, and he banned imports of French brandy. He lowered taxes on corn, thus making it cheaper to use, and liberalised distilling. In 1690, consent was given to a new law 'encouraging the distilling of brandy and spirits from corn'. As a result, anyone could make spirits out of British grain, as long as they paid a token customs fee and gave ten days' notice of their plans to begin distilling. It was a way of thanking his landowning supporters, since they now had a way to make additional profits from grain harvests. Surplus grain not needed for food use, or grain that was unsuitable for food, could be turned into cheap spirits. Consequently, landowners and farmers became closely involved with distillers and equally keen to promote the drinking of this new spirit, which became known as gin. Setting up a distillery was inexpensive, and the output could be huge, creating good profits. Over the next few years, hundreds of distilleries were founded, particularly in London. Cheap to make, gin was a drink that could be sold to a mass market. It was much lower in quality than genever, and was frequently adulterated.

While genever was still imported (and smuggled) for the benefit of the wealthy, gin became the drink of the poor. Gin's cheapness, scale of demand and level of adulteration highlighted social differences and it became the 'infamous liquor' leading to a period of mass intoxication on a scale that had never before been experienced: a poison and a blight on society.

Chapter 2

How The Gin Trade Developed

Although well intended, the decision to encourage sales of gin by helping landowners find new markets for their surplus grain proved to be disastrous. A low quality product, English gin was not regarded as a suitable alternative to Dutch genever. Genever drinkers simply sought out supplies of their favourite product, whereas gin was the drink of the poor. Criticism and opposition to the gin trade became so strong that eventually the government was forced to act – but so dire was the situation that it took decades to make any impact.

People had always got drunk, but what was different this time was the sheer scale involved. What made it so serious was the fact that people were almost continually inebriated. The cheapness of the gin made it accessible to people living at the edges of society, the poor, the deprived and the desperate. Going to the gin shop to buy a dram of gin for a penny was often the only entertainment or leisure activity available. Gin was cheaper than buying bread, and as a warming drink it gave some solace for a little while. The gin shop offered a measure of shelter, and was often more comfortable than the overcrowded, substandard buildings inhabited by these poverty-stricken people. An added advantage was the simple fact that gin was safer to drink than water, which was usually contaminated as it was sourced from streams and rivers that were also used to dispose of human and animal waste.

Rise of the gin shops

Gin was mainly sold from unlicensed premises, often in the backroom of a shop or a private home. Many gin shops offered a simple choice 'Drunk for a penny, Dead Drunk for Twopence. Clean Straw for nothing.' Other popular venues to buy gin were wine and spirit merchants trading from what became known as 'gin vaults'. Gin was also sold in taverns and alehouses, as well as all kinds of general shops like chandlers and grocery stores. It was sold under a variety of names including Cuckold's Comfort, Ladies Delight and Knock Me Down. There were also countless illegal stills and drinking dens, as well as casual sellers in the streets often carrying 'little double Dram-cup, which being held up on one side was a Penny, and on the other side a Half-penny'. Some employers partly paid wages in gin, or sold it to their employees. It was universally available.

Everyone drank gin – men, women and children. Women were excluded from alehouses and had to seek beverages elsewhere. The gin shop became the automatic alternative, especially since they could meet their friends there. Gin shops also attracted criminal elements, places where thieves and robbers could meet with fences (people who were happy to trade in stolen goods). It was also where drinkers drank to excess. A pamphlet entitled *Distilled Liquors: the Bane of Nations* stated:

> I am informed, in one place not far from East Smithfield, a Trader has a large empty Room backward, where as his wretched Guests get intoxicated, they are laid together in Heaps, promiscuously, Men, Women and Children until they recover their senses.

Although the effects of gin drinking were most noticeable in large towns and cities like London, it was common throughout the country. One observer wrote that there were 'convenient houses planted thick in every Village, where they have Gin in exchange for Coals, Candles, Small Beer, Bread and Cheese and Meat'. In Devon, The Salutation Inn constantly attracted attention from the official authorities. Newspapers like the *Western Times* refer to 'disgraceful proceedings at The Salutation' due to people imbibing 'a pint of gin' and 'large doses of opium'.

Producing and selling gin was undoubtedly profitable. The gin industry had been built on this need to serve the landed interest, and Daniel Defoe pointed out in 1713 that:

> The ordinary produce of corn in England is much greater than the numbers of our people or cattle can consume … The distilling trade is one remedy for this disaster as it helps to carry off the great quantity of corn in such a time of plenty, and it has this particular advantage, that if at any time a scarcity happens, this trade can halt for a year and not be lost entirely as in other trades it often happens to be … But in times of plenty and a moderate price of corn, the distilling of corn is one of the most essential things to support the landed interest than any branch of trade can help us to, and therefore especially to be preserved.

For many years, everything possible was done to encourage the development of distilling and the production of gin. All restrictions on its production were removed, and under the Mutiny Act of 1720, any retailers who were also distillers were able to avoid having soldiers quartered upon them.

A threat to law and order

Criticism of the deteriorating situation and the threat being posed to law and order became ever more vocal from 1721 onwards. The Westminster justices in 1721 stated that:

> Nor is there any part of this town wherein the number of alehouses, brandy and Geneva-shops do not daily increase, though they were so numerous already that in some of the largest parishes every tenth house at least sells one sort or another of those liquors by retail.

They concluded this was 'the principal cause of the increase of our poor and of all the vice and debauchery among the interior sort of people, as well as of the felonies and the disorders committed in and about this town'. In the same year, another committee of justices responding to fears of the plague was appointed to consider sanitary nuisances, which included 'persons retailing brandy, Geneva and other distilled liquors'. The committee noted that these were creating health risks due to:

> The great destruction made by brandy and Geneva-shops whose owners retail their liquors to the poorer sort of people and do suffer them to tippling in their shops, by which practice they are not only rendered incapable of labour ... (but by their bodies being kept in a continual heat) are thereby more liable to receive infection.

The decision to exempt distillers and retailers from quartering soldiers also came under attack by the justices who asked the Secretary of State for War to overturn the decision. They complained that every retailer operated a still and sold spirits, thus avoiding having to house soldiers. The justices believed that distillers and retailers should not be exempt, since these places caused 'more mischief and bad behaviour than any other type of business'. They added 'we are informed by several physicians' that these places are more likely 'to prepare and dispose of the bodies of those who usually drink such liquors ... to receive any infection that might be brought in among us.'

Excise and Revenue accounts from 1721 emphasised the scale of the problem. Approximately one-quarter of London's residents were reported to be employed in the production of gin, creating around 2 million gallons of tax-exempt product every year. Over the next ten years, gin consumption doubled again, with drinkers able to buy a dram of gin for a penny.

By 1725, the Chairman of the Middlesex Bench Justices made their complaints known, telling the Grand Jury that:

> The cry of excessive ... drinking of gin and other pernicious spirits, is become so great, so loud, so importunate, and the growing mischiefs from it so many, so great, so destructive of the lives, families, trades, and businesses of such multitudes, especially of the lower, poorer sort of the people, that I can no longer doubt but it must soon reach the ears of our legislators.

The growing tide of criticism began to bear fruit. In 1725, a committee of justices was appointed to assess the scale of the increasing number of retailers selling gin. After investigation, 6,187 houses and shops were identified within the metropolis (excluding the City of London and the Surrey side of the river) openly selling gin. Many combined selling gin alongside provision of other services and products. It stated:

> In some parishes every tenth house, in others every seventh, and in one of the largest, every fifth house, the committee believe it to be very far short of the true number, there being many who sell [gin] ... even in the streets and highways, some on bulks set up for that purpose, and others in wheelbarrows, and many more who sell privately in garrets, cellars, backrooms and other places ... The committee observe with deep concern the strong inclination of the inferior sort of people to these destructive liquors, and yet, if that were not sufficient all arts are used to tempt and invite them. All chandlers, many tobacconists, and such who sell fruit or herbs in stalls and wheelbarrows sell Geneva, and many inferior tradesmen begin now to keep it in their shops for their customers, whereby it is scarce possible for soldiers, seamen, servants or others of their rank, to go anywhere without being drawn in either by those who sell it or by their acquaintance,

whom they meet with in the street, who generally begin by inviting them to a dram … In the hamlet of Bethnal Green above forty weavers sell it.

The committee pointed out that it was causing major problems even in the workhouses. The justices noted that various drunken incidents had occurred, such as those at the workhouse in the parish of St Giles in the Fields. Even though gin was not officially allowed in the workhouse, 'Geneva is clandestinely brought in among the poor there, and they will suffer any punishment … rather than live without it, though they cannot avoid seeing the fatal effects of the deaths of those among them who had drunk most freely of it.' Four years later, the Grand Jury of Middlesex also complained about the problems caused by gin shops.

The gin problem is even mentioned in John Gay's *Beggar's Opera*, written in 1728. Peachum tells Mrs Trapes that 'one may know by your Kiss your Ginn is excellent' and Macheath, the captain of the robbers, demands women on whose lips he can taste gin, and hopes that they will 'be so free' as to choose gin for themselves because he loves 'a free-hearted wench'. Despite this, he later highlights the problems of gin, telling Betty that she should avoid gin and return to 'good wholesom Beer; for in troth, Betty, Strong-Waters will in time ruin your Constitution'. Further stress is placed on the harmful effects of gin when Lucy attempts to poison Polly. She points out that 'I run no risqué; for I can lay her death upon the gin, and so many die of that naturally that I shall never be called in question.'

Writing a pamphlet in 1726 on behalf of the London Company of Distillers entitled 'A Brief Case of the Distillers, and the Distilling Trade in England, Show how Far it is the Interest of England to Encourage the Said Trade', Defoe commented that 'the ordinary people are now so very satisfied with malt spirits, and especially with their new compositions, that they do not seek French brandy in such manner as they formerly did.'

In 1729, Parliament passed a Gin Act aiming to deal with gin retailing issues. Under the terms of the Act, all retailers were required to pay £20 for an excise licence, and spirits were taxed at a rate of 5 shillings per gallon. A fine of £10 was imposed on anyone hawking gin in the streets. It had little effect, and was openly defied. Most retailers simply ignored it and did not obtain the required licences. Farmers and landowners complained about the effect on corn sales, and in 1733 it was repealed.

Many of the stills used to distil the gin were located in crowded parts of London, resulting in justices of the peace complaining in 1730 that the stills gave rise to countless fires. Most gin was also adulterated. Writing in *Swindled from Poison Sweets to Counterfeit Coffee: the Dark History of the Food Cheats*, Bee Wilson comments: 'in the history of distilling, adulteration is the rule, not the exception. The trade had always been rife with diluters, "artificial Rectifiers" and "sophistictors" who would draw brandy from a turnip, or 'meliorate' spirits with green vitriol.' During the Gin Craze, the desire of the poor for penny drams of hooch drove both licit and black-market distillers to fabricate 'gin' from whatever grain or flavourings they could get. One recipe created by Vauxhall-based distillers Beaufoy, James & Co contained oil of vitriol, oil of almonds, oil of turpentine, spirits of wine, lump sugar, lime water, rose water, alum and salt of tartar. Turpentine was frequently used because it was a cheap alternative that mimicked the flavour of juniper berries.

Drunkenness on the scale experienced during the Gin Craze was regarded as frightening by the rest of society. When drunk, people were easily incited to riotous behaviour, it was not so much that they drank gin to excess, but rather the feeling that the drunken rioting could impact on law and order, government and the overall economy.

The case of Judith Dufour

The situation simply continued to deteriorate, and the story of Judith Dufour became a cause célèbre among opponents of the gin industry.

A silk spinner from Spitalfields, she was an avid gin drinker. Due to her neglect, her child had been taken from her and placed in the care of the local workhouse. One weekend, she reclaimed her 2-year-old child, Mary, from the workhouse and went with a friend, Sukey, to a nearby field and killed the child in order to pay for gin. On 27 February 1734, her subsequent statement was read out at her trial at the Old Bailey. It stated:

> On Sunday night we took the Child into the Fields, and stripp'd it, and ty'd a Linen Hankerchief hard about its Neck to keep it from crying, and then laid it in a Ditch. After that, we went together, and sold the Coat and Stay for a Shilling, and the Petticoat and Stockings for a Groat. We parted the Money and join'd for a Quartern of Gin.

Dufour was convicted of murder and hung from the gallows.

Gin retailing continues to rise in numbers

By 1735, the Middlesex Sessions had noted that the number of gin retailers had actually increased. There were now over ninety weavers in Bethnal Green selling spirits, and over 400 'inferior trades' including shoemakers, barbers, carpenters, tailors, dyers and labourers. In total, the Middlesex Sessions believed there were 7,044 gin retailers of which 4,939 were licensed and 2,105 were unlicensed. However, these numbers were by no means accurate. The official returns identifying the number of retailers in each parish were actually made by the constables – many of whom were also selling gin. The Middlesex Sessions went on to complain that the effects of such availability were proving extremely detrimental to the area. It pointed out that:

> As they generally employ many journeymen ... this liquor being always at hand ... they are easily tempted to drink

freely of it, especially as they can drink the whole week upon score, and too often without minding how fast the score runs against them; whereby at the week's end they find themselves without any surplusage to carry home to their families; which most of course starve or be thrown on the parish ... With regard to the female sex, we find that the contagion has spread even among them, and that to a degree hardly possible to be conceived. Unhappy mothers habituate themselves to these distilled liquors, whose children are born weak and sickly, and often look shrivel'd and old as though they had numbered many years. Others again daily give it to their children ... and learn them even before they can go, to taste and approve this certain destroyer.

As if that was not enough, the Middlesex Sessions expressed its concern about the impact on law and order in the area. They believed that gin was causing an upsurge in violent crimes since drinkers were 'carried to a degree of outrageous passion'. It pointed out that these 'poisonous liqours' left people 'in the streets in a condition abhorrent to reasonable creatures'. Children were left naked and starving, forced to beg or become a burden on the parish. Riots over gin were not unknown. In 1735, there are records of a riot involving the storming of a gin shop:

At Seven Dials occurred a Riot at the closing of a Gin Shop owned by Captain Speke. When the Mob became outrageous in their attempts to force the stoutly defended Building, Justice of the Peace Mr Maitland read the Riot Act but the Mob refused to disperse peaceably as required, the Guard of the Tower was called to enforce the Peace with Ball, Butt and Bayonet, after which all was quiet. The Shop was wrecked by Intruders and all the Genever Spirits lost.

The London Grand Jury was equally emphatic, presenting to the Lord Mayor a series of complaints about the 'late surprising Increase of Gin Shops and other Retailers of Distilled Spirituous Liquors.' Their petition pointed out that gin was robbing the 'lower kind of people' of their will and ability 'to labour for a honest livelihood, which is a principal reason of the great Increase of the Poor'. As a result, it caused 'such publick Nuisances as disturb and annoy the inhabitants of the City'.

Their comments were echoed in a report by the Grand Jury of the City of Westminster, stating that since gin was sold so cheaply:

> The meaner, though useful Part of the Nation, as Day Labourers, Men and Women Servants and Common Soldiers, nay even Children are enticed and seduced to taste, like and approve of these liquors, whereby they are intoxicated and get Drunk and are frequently seen in our Streets in such a Condition abhorrent to reasonable creatures ... are thereby rendered useless to themselves as well as the Community.

According to Daniel Defoe, compound distillers creating the actual gin were a major cause of problems within the gin industry at this time, commenting that they included many 'loose and disorderly persons' and

> they carry on their trade as if they were always drunk, keep no books but their slate, and no pen and ink but their chalk and tallies ... They are a collection of sinners against the people, for they break almost all the known laws of Government in the Nation.

The following year, the London Grand Jury added that 'Most of the Murders and Robberies lately committed have been laid and concentrated at Gin-shops' because drinkers 'being fired with these Hot Spirits ... are prepared to execute the most bold and daring Attempts.' The Middlesex Magistrates complained that they

> observe the strong inclination of the inferior Sort of people to these destructive Liquors, and how surprisingly this infection has spread within these few Years ... It is scarce possible for Persons in low life to go anywhere or be anywhere, without being drawn in to taste, and, by Degrees, to like and approve of this pernicious Liquor.

Thomas Wilson, the son of the Bishop of Sodor, published a pamphlet entitled *Distilled Spirituous Liquors: the Bane of a Nation*, asserting that 'gin was responsible for the General corruption of Servants, which every private Family feels and complains of', for the 'Idleness, Inability or Decrease of the Common people' and the increasing numbers of 'lazy sturdy beggars, street robbers and Housebreakers'. The desire for spirits was affecting all society since they had developed a taste for the liquor by the bad example of their masters. Wilson commented that in the south-eastern counties, farmers were responsible and that if servants return to their ancient simplicity, eating and drinking without one distiller in the kingdom, they would be able to pay their rents, and would not set a bad example to their servants. 'The evil is so Epidemick, that the greatest part of the nation, that Part which is the Strength and Riches of every Country, the Laborious hands, is intoxicated and enervated by a fatal Love of a slow but sure Poyson.'

As if such complaints were not strong enough to ensure action ought to be taken, a further issue was raised: that the impact of gin drinking would make it difficult to find men capable of serving in the army or navy. The London Grand Jury pointed out that 'The nation, (if obliged to enter into a war) will want strong and lusty soldiers, the Merchant sailors, and the Husbandman Labourers.' It was a message that resounded among the ruling classes. Sir Robert Walpole and Sir Joseph Jekyll both denounced gin for contributing to idleness and crime, and ensuring that the nation was unable to defend itself due to insufficient manpower.

Parliament tried again to impose some form of control. The Gin Act of 1736 introduced a duty of 20 shillings a gallon on spirits, while retailers were required to take out an annual licence costing £50. It was not a success. Only three licences were ever obtained, and the volume of spirits sold increased, reaching over 8 million gallons by 1743. Instead of controlling the trade, it increased illicit activity.

Even as the legislation was being passed, opposition was growing. Landowners complained that it would decrease their income. It was suggested that the act would destroy a trade and result in a £70,000 loss of revenue.

Popular protests

The Gin Act of 1736 led to popular protests. Recognising the possibility of dissent and riots, the prime minister, Sir Robert Walpole, doubled the number of guards on duty at St James, Kensington Palace and Whitehall. In Spitalfields, mobs took to the streets drinking the last legal gin available.

An illustration from the period, entitled *The Funeral Procession of Madam Geneva*, showed a mock 'procession through the London parish of St Giles, led by a group of distillers and a naked beggar'. Poor people look on in woe. The accompanying caption reads:

Now This Act, they cry, will lurch us
For Beer, a Quart's too great a Purchase
No tis resolved Divine Geneva!!
We'll bravely perish e'er we'll ever leave ye:
With that the brimming Glass they ply
And Poverty and Rags Defy ......

> How great those Patriots publick Spirit
> To strip the Poor of their Chief Pleasure
> And Thousands leave to Starve at Leasure.

Yet another illustration showed a tomb made from a still 'to the mortal memory of Madam Geneva'. Surrounding the tomb are groups of mourners comprising distillers, soldiers, poor women and children. In the centre of the print is a dedication:

> To the Mortal Memory of
> Madam Geneva.
> Who died Sept 29. 1736
> Her Weeping Servants &
> Loving Friends consecrate
> This Tomb.

A similar sentiment is portrayed in the *Lamentable Fall of Madam Geneva*, which contains the image of a man and woman standing over Madam Geneva's inebriated body, proclaiming her death as a mock deity. Lamenting, the woman complains that 'this act will starve us all', while the man has a sheet highlighting the miracles Madam Geneva has performed:

> Th' Afflicted she has caus's to Sing
> The cripple leap and Dance,
> All those who die for love of Gin
> Go to heaven in a Trance.

An accompanying verse highlights the impact it has on Madam Geneva's followers:

> With Oaths they storm their Monarch's name
> And curse the hands that form'd the Scheme

Queen Gin, for whom they'd Sacrifice
Their Shirts, or Smocks, nay both their Eyes…
They'd trudge the Street without their Shoes on.

Members of the government came under considerable criticism, and were described as hypocritical for being happy to get drunk themselves on wine and other alcoholic beverages but not allowing poorer people to drink their chosen beverage. The anonymous author of a satirical poem entitled *An Elegy on the Much Lamented Death of the Most Excellent, the Most Truly-Beloved and Universally Admired Lady, Madam Gineva* commented:

Howe'er they gloss their late officious Zeal,
With feigned Pretence to serve the Common-Weal!
Envy we know, this harsh Restraint suggest/
(O shy shou'd Envy enter Noble Breasts?)
Jealous that beggars with the Rich shou'd vie,
Dare to drink Drams and like their Betters Die'
Must we then lose alas! However loth,
The blissful Privilege of drunken Sloth?!
Freedom and Property are then but Names?
Th' injurious Parliament our birth-Right claims.

Even theatres became involved, with a farce being performed at The Haymarket celebrating 'The Deposing and Death of Queen Gin, with the ruin of the Duke Rum, Marquee de Nantz, and the Lord Sugarcane etc. … And Heroic-Comic-Tragical Farce.'
    In 1737, an anonymous document entitled *The Trial of the Spirits* was published which also noted:

The Strength and Riches of a National Community consist
in the Health and Numerousness of its Labourers … If
these be not preserv'd where will you find Soldiers? How

will the culture of your Lands, the useful Manufactures and
Merchandise of the Nation be carried on?

The author noted that it was not the fact that such drunkards could
not labour, and died early, but also forgot to pay debts, leaving others
out of pocket, and left their families in poverty:

> The Pigmy generation of Animals they leave behind them,
> unfit for Labour and industry … would rather see three
> half pence worth of gin, than a full Pot of Porter, or good
> wholesome Beer.

In addition, drinking gin created 'a false courage of Mock-Heroism'
resulting in crime and disorder, with 'desperate Attacks, Highway
and Street Robberies, attended sometimes with the most Cruel
and unheard of Murthers'. The author believed that such was the
strength of their passion for gin, 'the Fear of a House of Correction,
Imprisonment or Danger of the Gallows make little Impression upon
them, if any at all.'

The question of taxes and revenue was also raised. The writer
of *The Trial of the Spirits* pointed out that labouring people could
not spend their money on both beer and gin. This deprived the beer
industry and subsequently the Treasury of income, whereas gin
was raising very little duty. Gin drinking affected another revenue
generating industry: tobacco. He wrote:

> The consumption of tobacco, no inconsiderable a branch
> of His Majesty's revenue, and to which the populace do
> not a little contribute. An honest man may smoke a pipe
> or two of tobacco, with a pint or two of good beer, a whole
> evening, but is so suddenly demolish'd by the force of
> tyrant gin, that he has scarcely time to puff out half a
> dozen wiffs.

Loopholes in the law remained, resulting in the activities of Captain Dudley Bradstreet entering the history books as a result of his innovative method of selling gin. An Irish adventurer, soldier and secret government agent, he identified a legal loophole, which stated that informers must know the name of the person renting a property from which gin was being sold illegally. Without that information, justices of the peace did not have the authority to break into the premises in order to make an arrest. According to his autobiography, *The Life and Uncommon Adventures of Captain Dudley Bradstreet,* he arranged for a friend to rent a house in the City of London on Blue Anchor Alley. He then purchased in Moorfields a sign bearing an image of a cat and nailed it to a window overlooking the street. Bradstreet spent his remaining £13 on gin from Langdales Brewery, Holborn, informed everyone in the area that gin would be available at the sign of the cat on the following day and barricaded himself into the house.

'I then caused a Leaden Pipe, the small End out about an inch, to be placed under the Paw of the Cat, the End that was within had a Funnel to it,' he wrote. The next day he placed himself behind the sign and waited. It was a long wait, but then 'I heard the Chink of Money, and a comfortable Voice say, "Puss, give me two Pennyworth of Gin." I instantly put my Mouth to the Tube and bid them receive it from the Pipe under her Paw, and then measured and poured it into the Funnel, from whence they soon received it.'

Bradstreet's Puss and Mew system proved very popular, as Bradstreet explained:

> From all Parts of London People used to resort to me in such Numbers, Neighbours could scarcely get in or out of their Houses. After that manner I went on for a Month, in which time I cleared upwards of two and twenty pounds.

Within a short time, Puss and Mew was being copied throughout London. The authorities were powerless to act.

John Wesley, founder of the Methodist Church, commented that 'buying, selling and drinking of liquor, unless absolutely necessary were evils to be avoided'. He was not the only one to criticise the deteriorating situation. Countless other writers, churchmen, made similar comments.

The Gin Act encouraged people to become informers and report illegal distilling. In return, they were paid £5. Over 4,000 claims for this reward money were made following the 1736 Act. Most did not actually receive anything as the reward was linked to the fine paid by an offender. Many people simply could not afford the fine, so opted to go into the workhouse or prison instead. Although potentially lucrative, becoming an informer was also extremely hazardous. Reports from the period indicate that informers were chased and beaten to death by angry crowds. Informers were reviled, pelted with stones and dirt in the streets, and even thrown into the Thames. Some informers were even subjected to the 'skimmington rides' ritual normally used for cuckolded husbands. One informer was 'set upon an ass … while others beat and pelted him, leading him up and down Bond Street'. In August 1734, there are accounts of informers being thrown into a pond used to water horses, at Moor's Yard next to St Martin in the Fields. In 1738, a mob attacked the household of magistrate Sir Thomas De Viel, in Frith Street, Soho. Over 1,000 people were involved. Viel was forced to send for troops from St James to disperse the crowds threatening to hunt down informers.

Over the next few years, gin consumption began to rise again. The winter Frost Fairs held on the frozen River Thames for several years were renowned for selling a mix of gin and gingerbread to revellers. Contemporary prints show tents and stalls selling hot gin and gingerbread. Evidence began to appear of former evils such as excessive drunkenness, mortality and crime. There were reports of incidents nationwide such as people selling furnishings and even their homes to buy gin, a coachman pawning his wife for a quart bottle and a cattle drover selling his 11-year-old daughter to a trader for a bottle of gin. Complaints and calls for action against the gin industry had begun to mount. There were petitions to the House of Commons from the Corporation of London, local government authorities in Westminster and many London parishes, as well as the Bristol, Norwich and Manchester city authorities; all stressed the need to reduce the excessive use of spirits, claiming that gin was destroying people and lives, creating idleness, disorder and threatening trade.

In 1743, another Gin Act came into force, marking a reversal of the 1736 Act. Licences to sell gin became cheaper, costing just 20 shillings, but these licences could only be granted to people who already possessed an alehouse licence. Distillers were no longer allowed to retail gin. This measure did begin to reduce consumption.

The same year, Lord Hervey commented that 'the great fortunes recently made were to him a convincing proof that the trade of distilling was the most profitable of any now exercised in the kingdom except that of being broker to a prime-minister.'

Yet another Gin Act was introduced in 1747. This was due to distillers claiming they had experienced financial hardships and victimisation by informers. The distillers were given the right to retail gin as long as they obtained a licence costing £5.

Opposition to the gin trade

Henry Fielding was one of the most vocal opponents of the gin trade. A London magistrate and the founder of the Bow Street Runners, he was very much aware of its effects. Writing in the Enquiry into the Late Increase in Robbers, he stated:

> The drunkenness I here intend is that acquired by the strongest intoxicating liquors, and particularly by that poison called Gin which is ... the principal sustenance ... of more than an hundred thousand people in this metropolis ... the

dreadful effects of which I have the misfortune to every day
to see, and to smell too.

He pointed out that there were now believed to be 17,000 gin shops in
London and drinkers would use any means at their disposal to satisfy
their craving:

> The intoxicating draught itself disqualifies them from using
> any honest means to acquire it, at the same time that it removes
> all sense of fear and shame, and emboldens them to commit
> every wicked and desperate enterprise. Many instances of this
> I see daily; wretches are often brought before me, charged
> with theft and robbery, whom I am forced to confine before
> they are in a condition to be examined; and when they have
> afterwards become sober, I have plainly perceived … that
> Gin alone was the cause of the transgression.

Access to gin supplies was regarded as being extremely easy since
even the poorest lodging houses supplied gin on demand. Fielding
pointed out that:

> Mr Welch, high constable of Holborn stated that in the
> parish of St Giles and St George Bloomsbury lodging houses
> accommodated beds from cellar to garrett, price of double bed
> being no more than threepence; these places are no less provided
> for drunkenness, gin being sold in them all at a penny a quarter,
> so that the smallest sum of money serves for intoxication.

Fielding added a warning to the government as to the long-term
implications of the gin epidemic:

> What must become of the Infant who is conceived in Gin?
> What could an Edward or a Henry, a Marlborough or a

Cumberland, effect with an Army of such wretches? Doth not this polluted Source, instead of producing Servants for the Husbandman or Artificer; instead of providing Recruits for the sea or the Field, promise only to fill Alms-houses and Hospitals and to infect the Streets with Stench and Diseases?

The potential consequences of gin drinking were stressed in a verse in *The Lady's Magazine or the Universal Entertainer* in 1751 entitled 'Chalk'd' on the Shutters of an Infernal Gin-Shop':

> Briton! If thou would'st sure Destruction shun,
> From these curs'd walls, as from Serpent run;
> For there a Thousand Deaths in Ambush lie,
> Fatal to all, who dare approach too nigh.

Other campaigners pointed out the negative effects gin was having on the economy. In 1751, Isaac Maddox published a pamphlet entitled *Expediency of Preventative Wisdom*, focusing on the evils of labouring class gin consumption. While highlighting the problems gin was causing in terms of disorder and robberies, deaths and family life, he laid the greatest stress on the fact that by gin killing or rendering workers incapable, it deprived the nation of labour and consumption, as well as destroying businesses. Asking: 'How many Consumers of the general Product of the Nation are annually killed, and how many Commodities and how many Utensils does this pernicious Gin supplant or supply the place of?' Maddox compared the lives of gin lovers to those of more respectable workmen:

> Look in upon the dwelling of a regular industrious workman of the like Occupation of the slaves to Gin … many Trades have been employed to provide Cloaths and furnish a homely but decent and cleanly habitation for himself his Wife and healthy Children … the noisome, filthy abode of Gin

drinkers, if they have any settled abode at all, shall be void of everything decent or even necessary.

He believed that 'True Policy, Humanity and Religion' required governments to use their powers to ensure people led industrious and useful lives and regulate the consumption of gin by reforming the distilleries and raising the price of gin.

Campaigners were equally horrified that women were drinking gin to excess and the perceived effect this had on home life. Merely looking at the interior of a gin drinking wife's home reflected the level of neglect. Eliza Haywood, author of a pamphlet called *A Present for Women Addicted to Drinking Adapted to all the different Stations of Life, from a Lady of Quality to a Common Servant*, wrote:

> When you see the Kitchen in disorder, the Children half Naked and the House in a universal Litter, your Indignation will rise at the Thought of what Occasions it, You will, from that moment, look upon a Dram Glass, as a more dangerous Instrument than a Blunderbuss.

Perhaps the most influential – and well known – of all the criticisms of the gin industry was that of Hogarth, the influential artist. His 1751 compositions *Gin Lane* and *Beer Street* clearly showed the different results from drinking these two types of alcohol. It is a comparison of order and disorder, prosperity and ruin. Writing to a friend, Hogarth commented:

> In Gin Lane every circumstance of its horrid effects is brought into view ... idleness, poverty, misery and distress, which drives even to madness and death ... not a house in tolerable condition but the pawnbroker's and gin-shop. Beer Street, its companion, was given as a contrast, where the

invigorating liquor is recommended, in order to drive the other out of vogue.

He added in a letter to the *London Evening Post* that 'the subjects of these prints are calculated to reform some reining vices peculiar to the lower class of people'.

Gin Lane shows the destruction caused by gin. Set in the area around St Giles in central London, it shows the steeple of St George's church, Bloomsbury in the distance. It is a scene of total disorder. Centre stage is a drunken woman, clothed in rags, breasts exposed. She is so drunk that she does not realise that the child has slipped from her arms, and is falling over a railing to her death. Behind her townsfolk argue, and one man shares a bone with a dog. Roofs collapse into the street and houses are run down. An inebriated man beats himself over the head with a pair of bellows. There is a graveyard scene, with a burial underway. Gin is being peddled on a wheelbarrow. The streets are full of skeletal-like people with ribs showing, faces like skulls, bearing syphilis sores and some committing suicide.

Beer Street, on the other hand, shows a very different image as it sets out to show the advantages of beer drinking. It is an industrious scene, with people at work, happy and going about their normal lives. Houses are being built, businesses are operating, people sit comfortably and chat. They are well fed, well dressed and have well cared for children.

The two prints were accompanied by a poem written by Hogarth's friend Rev. James Townley stating:

Gin, cursed Fiend, with Fury fraught
Makes human Race a Prey
It enters by a deadly Draught
And steal our Life away.
Virtue and Truth, driv'n to Despair

Its Rage compels to fly,
But cherishes with hellish Care
Theft, Murder, Perjury.
Damned Cup! That on the Vitals preys
That liquid Fire contains,
Which Madness to the heart conveys,
And rolls it thro' the Veins

Beer, happy produce of our Isle
Can sinewy Strength impart
And wearied with Fatigue and toil,
Can cheer each manly Heart.

It was not until 1751 that a Gin Act became a law which actually made a difference, reducing the excesses of gin drinking. This Act strictly enforced the licensing requirements of the 1743 Act, increased the duty paid on spirits, and forbade distillers, chandlers and grocers to become involved in the retail of spirits. It encouraged the sale of 'respectable' gin by requiring that licences be granted only to people trading from premises rented for at least £10 per year. The specific mention of chandlers and grocers was a major step towards controlling consumption of gin because these were shops where gin was being sold along with food such as bread, small beer and cheese. Everyone visited these shops as it was the cheapest place to get breakfast, since food could be purchased by the ha'porth. By forbidding the sale of gin at these stores, it broke the chain of consumption. According to Dorothy George's *London Life in the Eighteenth Century* 'it was a turning-point in the social history of London and was so considered when this time was still within living memory.'

The types of gin being produced continued to vary considerably in quality. In 1757, Ambrose Cooper's the *Compleat Practical Distiller* contained a simple recipe for gin using 'three pounds of juniper berries, proof spirit ten gallons, water four gallons' for distillation.

Cooper also commented that the 'common sort of gins' are made using oil of turpentine and that 'it is surprising that people should accustom themselves to drinking it for pleasure'.

By 1760, Parliament had decided that the Act had been so successful in dealing with the problem and that 'the high price of spirits hath greatly contributed to the health, sobriety and industry of the common people' that duty was further increased. Over the next two decades, consumption of gin steadily declined, eventually reaching approximately 1 million gallons. By 1784, distillers were complaining that their income had been reduced, and that smuggling had increased. Duty was reduced the following year, and quickly resulted in a growth in consumption.

Yet another attempt was made to regulate the industry in 1769. This Gin Act banned distillation by small producers in London and placed high taxes on all other producers. It also abolished taxes on imports such as brandy in order to protect alliances with various European countries. On becoming law in March 1769, it was enforced immediately. People were arrested for selling and producing illicit gin.

The Gordon Riots of 1780 caused further problems in London. Lord George Gordon was a fervent Protestant, totally opposed to the measures easing the condition of Roman Catholics. His Protestant Association demanded the repeal of the 1778 Catholic Relief Act and he made numerous speeches whipping up anti-Catholic sentiment, spreading fear of 'popery', even suggesting that 20,000 Jesuits were hiding in tunnels below the River Thames ready to attack London. Eventually, Lord George Gordon led a mob of 10,000 people through the city destroying Catholic-owned property. Langdale's Black Swan Distillery on Holborn Hill was one of the buildings which came under attack as the owner, Mr Langdale, was known to be a Catholic. Attacking the distillery, they broke in, started drinking the gin and set fire to the building, causing damage worth over £50,000. Mr Langdale escaped through the back of the distillery. It was reported at the time that as fire raged through the distillery, gin started flowing down the street.

Rioters were seen desperately scooping up the gin and drinking it. Many drank themselves senseless and burnt in the flames.

It was an event which stayed in people's memories for a long time, affecting the way gin was regarded. Horace Walpole wrote a letter commenting: 'Religion has been the clock of injustice, outrage and villainy; in our late tumults, it scarce kept on its mask a moment; its persecution was downright robbery, and it was so drunk, that it killed its banditti faster than they could plunder.' Fifty years later, Lord Macaulay told MPs during a debate on universal education that they should 'count up all the wretches who were shot, who were hanged, who were crushed, who drank themselves to death at the rivers of gin which ran down Holborn Hill.'

Charles Dickens graphically describes the event in his novel *Barnaby Rudge,* which is set around the time of the Gordon Riots. He writes: 'the streets were now a dreadful spectacle. The shouts of the rabble, the shrieks of women, the cries of the wounded, and the constant firing, formed a deafening and an awful accompaniment to the sights which every corner presented.'

Gin drinking continued to be linked to crime and disorder. In 1792, Patrick Colquhoun, a magistrate in the city of London, was tasked with exploring the 'present state of the morals of the Metropolis'. In 1796, he published his conclusions in *A Treatise on the Police of the Metropolis: Containing a Detail of the Various Crimes and Misdemeanours By which the Public and Private Property and Security are, at present, injured and endangered: And suggesting Remedies for their Prevention.* It contained a summary of the groups he regarded as being 'the various classes of individuals who live idly and support themselves by pursuits that are either criminal, illegal, dissolute, vicious or depraved' together with their estimated numbers. Gin was placed high on his list coming in at No 23 as 'Grubbers, Gin-drinking dissolute women, and destitute Boys and Girls ... Who are constantly on the watch to pilfer when an opportunity offers ... 2,000'.

Campaigners also maintained their criticism of gin as being an unsuitable beverage. Hannah Moore's *The Gin Shop, or, A Peep into a Prison* (1795) pointed out that the gin shop was aligned with 'gaming-tables, Night-Houses, Bawdy-Houses' and that 'most private Shops in and about London (as there are too many) where Geneva is publickly sold in Defiance of the Act of Parliament, are filled with Whores, Thieves and Beggars'. She goes on to state:

> The State compels no man to drink,
> Compels no man to game;
> 'Tis GIN and gambling sink him down
> To rags, and want, and shame.

While the worst of the Gin Craze was over by the end of the eighteenth century, the problems remained, leading to yet more criticism in future decades.

Chapter 3

Gin Smuggling

Stories about smugglers landing goods on deserted beaches, crossing lonely moorlands with heavily laden pack ponies and having fights with excise men have entered folklore. Yet this is nothing new, especially when it comes to gin.

Smuggling gin has a long history. In medieval times, a group of Dutch and Flemish merchants working in the extremely lucrative wool trade established their headquarters in the Wiltshire town of Swindon. These merchants liked drinking Hollands (another name for gin or genever), but as high import duties made the drink very expensive, the merchants frequently smuggled barrels of Hollands among their trading goods. By the mid-sixteenth century, they had established a very successful smuggling ring. Barrels of alcohol were landed in quiet locations along the Hampshire coast, before being brought up to Swindon at night. As the journey was too long to accomplish in one trip, barrels were hidden during the day in church crypts or village ponds. According to one local legend, revenue men spotted the smugglers raking a pond for kegs. When asked what they were doing, the smugglers pretended to have lost their wits and said they were trying to take a piece of the moon that had fallen from the sky. Laughing, the revenue men left them to it.

The smuggling of illicit spirits continued throughout the seventeenth and eighteenth centuries and was a common occurrence due to the imposition of high taxes on desirable goods including genever, rum, brandy and tea. These items were often up to five times cheaper in continental countries compared to Britain. Such a difference in price became extremely significant in the scale of smuggling activity, especially when Dutch genever was regarded as much better quality than inferior home-distilled gin. Smuggled goods arrived in large increasingly large quantities.

Smuggling could be extremely violent. The Hawkshurst Gang was one of the most notorious of all smuggling gangs operating along the south coast. They took part in many battles with the excise, and were often seen at the Mermaid Inn, Rye with loaded weapons on the table. In 1744, the excise men were unable to stop them when they unloaded contraband from three ships at Pevensey on to 500 pack horses. Four years later, a farm worker was found dead in a lake at Parham Park, having been interrogated and beaten to death by the gang when they accused him of stealing contraband.

Joss Snelling was a notorious Kentish smuggler, whose gang was involved in what became known as the Battle of Botany Bay in 1769. The excise men discovered Snelling's gang bringing up barrels from the beach, and a battle ensued using guns, cutlasses, knives and boathooks as weapons. Snelling lost fifteen men in the battle. He escaped and was not captured until 1803. When captured he claimed he had come across the contrabrand by accident and was released.

In Norfolk, Parson Woodforde at Weston Longville kept a diary noting all aspects of life within his rural community. His entries show the frequency with which he received goods from the smugglers, although he did not provide them with direct assistance. In March 1777, Woodforde wrote:

> Andrews the smuggler brought me this night about 11 o'clock a bag of Hyson Tea 6 pound weight. He frightened us a little by whistling under the parlour window just as we were going to bed. I gave him some Geneva and paid for the tea at 10/6 a pound.

Woodforde also noted that he purchased gin and brandy from Richard Andrews as well as Clerk Hewitt of Mattishall Burgh, and Richard Moonshine Buck, the blacksmith at Honingham. Not all the smugglers he used were named. There were occasions noted in his diary when Parson Woodford simply received a knock at the door and by the time he reached it, the smuggler had vanished – leaving behind kegs waiting for bottling.

It is recorded that approximately 4 million gallons (17 million litres) of genever were produced in Holland in 1779, purely for the black market in England. The remote Robin Hood's Bay in Yorkshire was one of the key entry points and was known to be one of the richest villages on the east coast in the late eighteenth and early nineteenth century. Local historian and guide Paul Johnston says 'To an extent it was an entire village operation. There were several core families involved who you didn't mess around with.' So many of the villagers were involved that it was possible to move smuggled goods from the bottom of the village to the top without those goods ever appearing in daylight. Goods were landed at night in the small harbour, and quickly whisked through a maze of interlocking cellars, tunnels and trapdoors. The Mariners Tavern on the quayside was the centre of the village smuggling business, and the customs officers feared to visit it. Other taverns in the village were also involved. A local shop owner known to be involved in the smuggling trade became so wealthy that he was able to pay for the building of a Methodist chapel in the village, following a visit by John Wesley to the area.

The smugglers of Robin Hood's Bay were often quick to defend their illicit trade. Saltersgate Inn on the moors near Pickering was a known meeting point for smuggling gangs. It had a fire burning on the hearth that was never allowed to go out, since underneath the stone hearth lay the body of a customs officer killed by one of the smuggling gangs. Another Robin Hood's Bay smuggler was George 'Stoney' Fagg who dominated the coastal area from Whitby to Scarborough. His schooner, *The Kent*, was armed with sixteen 4-pounder guns incorporating twelve swivels. The revenue cutters were outgunned and no match for him. In 1777, Fagg was so confident in his abilities that he invited the revenue men on board the vessel while trading with ships in Bridlington Bay. On seeing a revenue cruiser nearby, he sent a message asking how they were doing for provisions. On hearing that gin stocks were low, Fagg invited them on to his ship for a drink and then sent them back with a free, half anker sample of gin. A few weeks later, the revenue men managed to muster a large force of ships and closed in on *The Kent* at Filey. When ordered to 'heave to or we fire', Fagg responded with the words 'Fire away, you bouggers, and be dammed to you.' Battle commenced and *The Kent* tried to flee. With other naval vessels arriving to take part, *The Kent* was outgunned. Fagg put his men in rowing boats, and ordered them to tow the ship as there was insufficient wind. Eventually he was forced to surrender, and *The Kent* was sailed into Hull by the revenue men, leading to 200 tonnes of contraband being unloaded at the customs warehouse.

In October 1779, Yorkshire revenue officers, backed by the militia, raided the Fisherman's Arms pub in Robin Hood's Bay, having received word that there was contraband in the cellars. They seized 200 casks of gin and brandy, 150 sacks of tea, plus an armoury of blunderbusses and cartridges. According to local legend, the customs men left to guard it overnight could not resist sampling the spirits, drank too much and fell asleep. Noticing this, the smuggling gang returned and quietly removed most of the contraband.

The outbreak of the French Revolution in 1779 made an already edgy situation for smugglers even tenser. The call of '*Liberté, égalité, fraternité*' aroused fear across Europe. There was a fear that the common people would rise up against the government and aristocracy just as they had done in France. Ever greater attention was paid to the activities of smugglers, fearing that they may be bringing in more than just illicit cargo, and potentially creating a threat to law and order within the country. Many smugglers were operating large networks and showed little concern for the excise.

Isaac Gulliver was one such very wealthy smuggler, who eventually built up an estate of £60,000 together with numerous properties. He owned a pub jointly with his father-in-law, William Beale, and invested money in carriers and outlets throughout Hampshire and Devon. As a smuggler, he was extremely successful operating fifteen luggers illegally transporting gin, silk, lace and tea. Known locally as the 'king of the Dorset Smugglers' and 'the gentle smuggler who never killed a man', his activities resulted in considerable local renown.

Writing in the early nineteenth century, historian George Roberts from Lyme Regis reported local stories that Gulliver

> kept forty or fifty men constantly employed who wore a kind of livery, powdered hair and smock frocks, from which they attained the name of 'White Wigs'. These men kept together and would not allow a few officers to take what they were carrying when the law was altered and seizures made from smaller parties. Gulliver amassed a large fortune and lived to a good old age. A chamber open towards the sea at the mouth of the River Lyme, was in existence where the White Wigs took refreshment and remained in waiting until their services were required. This was about one hundred yards from the Custom House.

Gulliver built numerous large houses such Howe Lodge, Kinson, in Bournemouth, which when demolished over a century later was found to include numerous hiding places such as a secret room accessible through a door hidden 10 feet up a chimney. There are reports that the customs men tried to arrest him but his wife told them he had just died, and showed them the 'body'. After they left, Gulliver got out of the coffin and escaped, leaving the coffin to be filled with stones and a mock funeral held.

In a report dated 1788 from the Custom House in Poole, the Commissioners of Customs in London were told that:

> Gulliver was considered one of the greatest and most notorious smugglers in the west of England and particularly in the spirits and tea trades but in the year 1782 he took the benefit of His Majesty's proclamation for pardoning such offences and as we are informed dropped that branch of smuggling and afterwards confined himself chiefly to the wine trade which he carried on to a considerable extent having vaults at various places along the coast and 'in remote places'.

As war with France became a reality by the 1790s, excise taxes increased still further, especially with regard to the sought-after, high quality, Dutch genever. Increasing numbers of fishermen took on an extra role, slipping over to France and Holland to obtain illicit quantities of such highly desirable merchandise.

Even in wartime, there was considerable collusion between the various participants across national boundaries. Fishermen and traders frequently met up with their compatriots in France, Holland and elsewhere to move goods from ship to ship in mid-channel, or simply pay a visit to foreign port to buy the required items. In France, Napoleon established warehouses to serve the needs of cross-channel smugglers. These were initially established at Dunkirk, but due to the rowdiness of the English smugglers, the trade was switched to the beach at Gravelines. New gin distilleries such as that of Distillerie Perseyn were set up in northern France, specifically to cater for the smuggled trade in illicit spirits.

Although a very profitable trade, smuggling was also potentially dangerous both for smugglers and excise men. It was not an easy life for the excise men. Their task was unpopular and they could not count on much support from the local authorities. They were also few in number. In many cases, just one excise man might be responsible for many miles of coastline. They could call on the help of the militia, but the potential temptation for all concerned was huge. In 1794, excise men found smugglers landing 500 barrels of gin on a Sussex beach. With the help of nearby troops, they dispersed the smugglers and captured the cargo. En route to the Shoreham customs house, two of the soldiers sampled the gin and were found comatose on the beach next morning. One of the soldiers was due to be married that day, but never recovered from his drinking bout.

Smuggling was undoubtedly big business. The potential profits involved were extremely high. It was not unusual for smugglers to return from the Continent with around 3,000 gallons of genever. Illegally imported gin was so common in Kent that there were reports that some villagers were using it to clean windows.

The scale of smuggling in Scotland was so great that on the Isle of Cumbrae, the town of Millport was established in the mid-1700s to stop goods being smuggled illegally through the Clyde estuary. High taxes on the 'necessities' of life such as alcohol, spices, lace, salt, tea, coffee and silks meant that such items became sought-after cargo. In 1845, the Clyde Revenue Service stationed its revenue cutter, the *Royal George,* at Millport to chase and examine suspect vessels. The cutter possessed sixteen guns and was manned by a crew of sixty men, mostly local sailors from Cumbrae. When smuggler ships were seized for possessing illegal goods, the excise men were permitted to keep a bounty and the town quickly became very wealthy, as seen by the large houses built by the shipowners. Despite this strong involvement with the excise, anecdotal reports indicated that Cumbrae was also popular with smugglers. Sailors were popular visitors to coastal farms due to the items they carried in their knapsacks, and it was said that there were occasions when Communion had to be postponed since smugglers had not been able to provide enough wine in time for the service to be held.

The eastern coast of Scotland was particularly popular with genever smugglers. Over 1,000 ankers of foreign spirits were landed illegally in Aberdeenshire every month – an anker being the equivalent to around 10 gallons. Due to the presence of extensive cave networks on the beaches, Collieston in Aberdeenshire was a haven for smugglers.

On 1 December 1798, the northern part of the beach at Cransdale was the scene of an extremely brutal battle between Philip Kennedy, a notorious gin smuggler, and the excise, when a lugger known as the *Crooked Mary* landed 16 ankers of gin. Kennedy was responsible for unloading the alcohol before moving it inland. The excise men had been tipped off and lay in wait armed with swords near Kirk of Slains. Kennedy went on ahead to check that the route was clear, and was attacked by the waiting excise men. During the fight, an excise man struck Kennedy on the head with a blow that cleaved his skull open. According to local records, Kennedy managed to stagger a quarter of a mile to the Kirk of Slains, where he collapsed and died. So ingrained in local memory was Kennedy's story that novelist Sir Walter Scott used it as inspiration for his novel *Guy Mannering*. Duncan Harley later reported in his book, *A to Z of Curious Aberdeenshire*, that Philip Kennedy's skull had been dug up several times over the years and was instantly identifiable by the deep cut caused by the excise man's sword.

Also in Scotland, where excise men were known as gaugers, William Alexander, a journalist writing in the nineteenth century, noted that the excise men were regarded as 'a fit subject for rough handling as occasion offered. To tie his legs together and fasten his hands forcible behind his back and leave him lying helpless on the lone hillside was not deemed out of place by any means.'

There was actually a shortage of money in the Shetland Islands between 1796 and 1798 due to the fact that so much money was being paid out by merchants to buy gin. The minister of Uist reported that gin imports were worth half the rents of the island. Other local accounts stated that illicit gin had 'drained the poor of this country ... of every shilling they could raise'. It was understandable – a fisherman might only earn 5 shillings per week and that represented the duty on a cask of spirits. Profit margins varied according to duty levels. A typical barrel of gin might cost £1, and customers would often pay £4, before diluting to a drinkable strength for wider distribution. Being involved in the smuggling trade could triple or quadruple this in the space of one night.

Equally inventive was a story about a smuggler in Lyme Regis, Dorset, who according to legend, encountered a senior excise man while carrying two large tubs of illicit liquor. The smuggler quickly put them down, and warmly greeted the excise man saying 'an excise man asked me to take these two tubs to you, gave me 2 shillings for the job, but if I'd known how heavy they were, I wouldn't have touched them.' Unable to carry the tubs himself, the senior excise officer gave him a florin and ordered him to bring them to the customs house, before walking off to await their arrival. Needless to say, the smuggler quickly disappeared with the tubs.

Not all the encounters were as amicable as this. There are countless tales from all round the coast concerning battles taking place between the smugglers and the excise men, including one from the early 1800s, when a boat full of excise men was found on the Sunken Island near Mersea in Essex. All had their throats cut.

A major incident occurred on 10 February 1805 at Sennen, Cornwall, a mile north-east of Land's End. The excise men seized 1,000 gallons of genever, rum and brandy from local smugglers. A fight resulted and shots were fired. A local man, John George, was captured, tried at the Old Bailey in London on 24 April, and sentenced to the gallows.

Smuggling was common throughout the British Isles from Kent to Aberdeen, from the West Country to Glasgow and beyond. On the Isle of Man, produce was imported legally on to the island by paying a small tariff to the Lord of Man, before being moved illegally across to Scotland, Ireland and the North of England. In Scotland, the Rotterdam Gentry was responsible for gin smuggling. They gained this name because Rotterdam was the centre of the gin trade. Their colleagues, the Hamburg Gentry, focused mainly on other items such as tea and brandy and only smuggled a small amount of gin.

Official records on the Shetland Isles reveal just how the Shetland Islanders combined smuggling with legitimate trading. In 1814, a ship named *The Catherine* began a trading voyage from Orkney. It loaded an illegal cargo of meal which it took to Bergen. The meal was unloaded, and replaced with a legal cargo of hides and tallow. These products were then delivered to London and replaced with a legal cargo of rope. *The Catherine* then headed to Rotterdam and added an illegal cargo of 600 ankers of gin. The gin was transported to Shetland and the rope taken to Orkney. Other similar trips were planned, but the smugglers were caught and the vessel seized at Kirkwall.

At Chideock and Burton Bradstock in Dorset, almost every family was believed to be involved in the smuggling trade. In 1820, excise man Samuel Dawson searched the premises of Chideock Mill and found two casks of brandy and two casks of genever under the miller's living quarters. The local vicar of Chideock, Rev. C. V. Godard later wrote:

> The fishing industry seems to have slipped away with the dwellings at Seatown. Some say that the fish have left the coast, but others (with whom I agree) say that in the old days the fishermen lived more by smuggling than by fishing. They were a hardy lot, and one of them, himself engaged in the trade as a youth, recalls the smuggling yarns that he, as a little boy, used to hear them tell and the adventures in which he later took part. There were wild rushes to the West Rocks (beneath Golden Cap) when a boat-load of spirits was being rowed ashore from a ship lying out at sea, each man readily shouldering his share of the load – two small kegs and scrambling off as fast as his legs would carry him. He would

find his own way inland to a safe retreat. Cranborne Chase, being a wild, uninhabited district, and the central moors of Dorset, were favourite hiding places.

Genever smuggling reached its peak in 1815 as the Napoleonic Wars came to an end. Many of the soldiers returning from the continental wars were recruited into the excise department and a new Coastal Blockade Service (later renamed the Coastguards). This made it much more hazardous for the smugglers to operate, at a time when lower taxes and import duties were reducing the potential profits.

Demand for smuggled goods was widespread across all sectors of society. Often the activities and identities of the smugglers were well known. Landowners and gentry turned a blind eye to the illegal trade, and willingly purchased the goods. The smugglers brought in vast quantities of gin, silk, brandy and salt, moving it across country in quiet pack trains in the dark of night. Horses' hooves were wrapped in cloths to reduce noise. Villagers who happened to see them passing by simply turned their faces away. This meant they could not be arrested for conspiring with the smugglers since hearing was not proof.

Although written many years later, the well-known poem by Rudyard Kipling reflects the attitudes so common at this time:

> If you wake at midnight, and hear a horse's feet,
> Don't go drawing back the blind, or looking in the street,
> Them that ask no questions isn't told a lie.
> Watch the wall my darling while the Gentlemen go by.
>
> Five and twenty ponies,
> Trotting through the dark –
> Brandy for the Parson, 'Baccy for the Clerk.
> Laces for a lady; letters for a spy,
> Watch the wall my darling while the Gentlemen go by!

If you meet King George's men, dressed in blue and red,
You be careful what you say, and mindful what is said.
If they call you 'pretty maid' and chuck you 'neath the chin,
Don't you tell where no one is, nor yet where no one's been!

Tales of ghosts started to increase around this time since it was an ideal way for smugglers to hide their activities. Historic UK reports that at Hadleigh Castle in Essex, two ghosts – the White Lady and the Black Man – appeared dramatically just before a shipment of illicit liquor arrived, and disappeared just as quickly once the shipment had been safely moved on. Tales of the Ghostly Drummer at Herstmonceux Castle, Sussex are also believed to have started when some enterprising smugglers used phosphorus to create a ghostly figure.

On arrival in Britain, the smuggled goods were immediately hidden in all kinds of locations from barns to holes in the ground. In Aberdeenshire, for example, pits lined with brick and timber were often dug 6ft or more into the sand, before being covered with both dry and wet sand to hide all traces. In Eyemouth, near Edinburgh, a smuggler named John Nisbet built a huge house known as Gunsgreen Mansion (now a smugglers' museum) which includes a vast hidden cellar, hidden passageways and even hidey holes for illicit goods in the walls and floors of the house.

Many landowners also helped hide the contraband, as well as buying it. Thorpe Hall, near the village of Fylingthorpe on the moors above Robin Hood's Bay, was owned by the Fawside family – known to be involved with the smuggling trade – who built an underground chamber near the fishpond. The local smugglers used it to leave a regular supply of alcohol for Mr Fawside's use.

At Great Holland, near Clacton in Essex, a farmer was known to be very fond of high quality gin. This was supplied by a group of London smugglers who used the area to bring in their illicit cargo.

The farmer simply asked them to 'leave the lane gate locked' to signal his barrel of gin was running low. In return, the farmer provided stabling for the smugglers' fifteen horses.

Smugglers became ever more inventive, digging out tunnels and passages to move cargos from remote bays. Barrels of spirits were often stored by sinking them offshore and then removed when the excise men left the area. Another frequently used option was to make rafts out of the barrels and allow them to float in on the surf. A painting by J.M.W. Turner, *Folkestone from the Sea* shows a group of English smugglers receiving barrels of illicit gin from French sailors by moonlight. With the onset of sunrise, the smugglers are spotted and a customs' boat approaches, leading the smugglers to 'sink' the barrels into the sea on open ropes for future retrieval.

In 1817, a notable sea battle occurred between the revenue cutter *Ranger* and a heavily armed smugglers' lugger. The battle raged from Robin Hood's Bay and along the east coast as far as Great Yarmouth, where the smugglers eventually abandoned their ship. During the fight, two smugglers and three revenue men were killed, while another seven revenue men were seriously wounded. A reward totalling £500 was offered, but the smugglers were never captured. Their financial losses were considerable as the contraband cargo and ship together was worth £10,000. The cargo contained 507 ankers and 945 half-ankers of genever, plus 206 bags of tea, 9 boxes of playing cards, 24 bales of tobacco and 47 bales of silk handkerchiefs.

The number of people participating in the smuggling trade was extensive. Many luggers involved crews of two or three dozen sailors. Unloading was equally labour intensive. At Boulmer, Northumberland, the landlord of the local pub owned a smuggling lugger. While waiting for the ship to return to port, the people responsible for carrying the goods across the region regularly hid in the nearby dunes. They emerged when the signal was given – a piper parading around the village playing 'O but ye've been lang awa'. Ye're welcome back again.'

The scale of smuggling at Boulmer was so extensive that the village was regarded as the smuggling capital of the area. During a battle with the excise, a local man named Wull Faa was seriously injured. When Faa, who was also a boxer and violinist, fought back using a cudgel against the excise man's cutlass, his cudgel was steadily whittled to a matchstick and his right hand was cut to the bone. He surrendered, complaining that his bow hand had been spoilt, resulting in a verse in local folk song noting:

> This is the canny Will Faa o' Kirk Yetholm,
> He lives at the sign o' the Queen;
> He got a great slash i' the hand
> When coming' frae Boulmer wi' gin'.

Over at Hawick, smuggler Alexander Mitchell was staying at the Carter Toll Bar with his father on his way back from Boulmer when he saw customs' men approaching. Mitchell had hidden illicit gin in the hayloft and the duo promptly ran up to guard it. A battle ensued, with Mitchell and his father succeeding in fighting off the customs' men. Afterwards, the father commented that, 'A've left the marks o' ma teeth on yin o' their legs at ony rate,' to which his son responded, 'it was me ye bate, father!'

If captured, the penalties for smuggling could be severe. Participants might be flogged, jailed, transported or hung on the gallows. Equally brutal was the treatment of the informants used by the excise to discover the activities of smugglers.

In Scarborough, intelligence provided by an informant led to the seizure of a boat-load of barrels in 1822. The smugglers rowing them in from an offshore lugger escaped but lost one boat-load of gin. When asked by the customs authorities for information about the smugglers, a man named Billy Mead named a wool merchant called James Law. Although Law was a smuggler, he claimed that this particular load of gin was not his responsibility and that Mead was lying. The legal proceedings were eventually heard in the Kings Bench in London, where Law won his case. Mead was found guilty of perjury and the smugglers sought revenge. Their chosen target was a local woodman named James Dobson, who had given evidence in the lawsuit against James Law. On 13 February 1823, Dobson came to the market in Scarborough, where he was greeted by a mob of angry people and beaten. His ribs were broken and he was rolled in a dog kennel and paraded through the town, tied to a ladder. Dobson would probably have died during the attack but for the intervention of a couple of local farmers who managed to rescue him and take him to safety.

For some smugglers, old habits remained, as the story of Joss Snelling reveals. Having been involved in smuggling since the 1760s, including taking part in the Battle of Botany Bay, he remained involved in smuggling all his life, together with his son and grandson. Snelling was fined £100 for smuggling in 1830 – he was aged 89 at the time. He was even presented to the future Queen Victoria as the 'famous smuggler' when she visited Broadstairs.

Chapter 4

Gin's Progress Through
The Nineteenth Century

As the nineteenth century dawned, little seemed to have changed. Gin was still the main tipple for most working-class people, and its links with crime and poverty continued. As the century progressed, the gin shop changed into something much more elaborate, often attracting a wider clientele as well as social observers assessing the state of society. The gin palace was born – but signs of changing attitudes were emerging. Although gin slowly gained respectability, the work of the Temperance Movement began to challenge opinions on alcohol.

The condition of England

As the century progressed, criticism of the evils of gin became ever stronger with issues of alcoholism becoming an integral part of the 'condition of England', an issue explored by numerous reformers like Charles Booth and Joseph Rowntree. The Temperance Movement was extremely vocal on the subject, attacking gin as a source of corruption, whereas beer was seen as a healthy drink with meals, causing less drunkenness. Children were recruited to the Band of Hope, pledging, 'I do agree that I will not use intoxicating liquors as a beverage.' It was extremely popular, with thousands of children taking the pledge. In one example of the Band of Hope's popularity, an 1852 meeting held at Exeter Hall in the Strand was attended by 6,000 participants. When thousands more turned up, they had to be shut out of the hall. The sheer weight of numbers stopped the traffic in the Strand.

George W. M. Reynolds was particularly critical of the depravity associated with gin, devoting considerable editorial to the issue in his series featuring Richard Markham in *The Mysteries of London*. Meeting three girls aged 11, 13 and 14 attempting to work out how much money they have left to purchase some gin, Markham decides:

> For Gin is the deity, and Intemperance is the hand-maiden, of both sexes and nearly all ages in that district of London. What crimes, what follies have been perpetrated for Gin! A river of alcohol rolls through the land, sweeping away health, honour, and happiness with its remorseless tide. The creaking gibbet, and the prison ward – the gloomy hulk, and the far-off penal isle – the debtors' gaol, and the silent penitentiary – the tomb-like workhouse, and the loathsome hospital – the galling chain, and the spirit-breaking tread-wheel – the frightful mad-cell, and the public dissecting-room – the death-bed of despair, and the grave of the suicide, are indebted for many, many victims to thee, most potent Gin!

Gin Shops

Wealth and poverty existed side by side in London, particularly within the West End. Only a short walk from Piccadilly, the home of elegant shops and the theatreland of Covent Garden, were the rookeries of Seven Dials or St Giles, where poverty and crime predominated. This was the area known as Rat's Castle or the Holy Land and contained thousands of people crammed into a small area. Twenty-four hour drinking was common, with gin shops serving the evening and night-time theatre staff, as well as the early morning market trade, followed by the daily trade. In 1816, Minutes of Evidence before a select committee recorded that one such house, known as The Finish, possessed a 'debauched clientele, [who] clammy from gin and pallid in the early morning light, seemed as ghouls, either raised from or immediately destined for the grave.'

Although gin shops had decreased in number since the Gin Craze of the previous century, they still existed and catered for a wide audience. Many gin shops still traded out of the backroom of a shop or a private home. A typical example was that of Mrs Knapman's gin shop in St Thomas, Exeter. Mrs Elizabeth Knapman was a widow and the gin shop provided her with an income. In 1838, a neighbour complained about the noise, 'there being but a slight partition dividing the shop from the sitting-room of the dwelling-house'.

Gin shops were not only places that sold cheap drink, but were frequently very unsavoury places. *The Spectator* noted, 'We cannot shut our eyes to the vast increase of crime, which has been solely attributed to those haunts of vice and ruin, the gin-shops.' Magistrates were still referring to people being led astray by gin, and encountered accusations of people having their pockets picked while drinking gin or picking up prostitutes. A popular song in the early nineteenth century contained the words:

> The drunkard sunk more in disgrace,
> Had a look of brutality scowling,
> In his soul, in his heart, in his face,
> The Gin like a demon was howling.

Prints were frequently published showing the depravity to be experienced in gin shops. George Cruikshank's illustration of 1820, *The Gin Shop*, was typical. The print shows a brightly lit, elaborate gin shop in which a mother is pouring gin into a baby's mouth, while her young daughter is drinking a glass of gin. Surrounding them are symbols of death including a gamekeeper's gin trap. *The Drunkard's Children*, also by Cruikshank, shows a girl committing suicide by jumping from a bridge into the Thames. The print is captioned with

the words 'The maniac father and the convict brother are gone –
The poor girl, homeless, friendless, deserted, destitute, and gin-mad,
commits self murder.' By 1834, Cruikshank was becoming even more
vocal on the subject. His satirical illustration, *The Gin-Juggernath*,
was based on images of wheeled statues of the Hindu god Jagannath.
The illustration shows a massive Juggernath being wheeled along on
barrels of gin, under which devotees threw themselves.

Gin Dens

The popularity of gin drinking dens in central London was further
emphasised in the adventures of a society duo. Egan, a jobbing hack,
worked with Cruikshank on an illustrated serial entitled '*Life in
London or The Day and Night Scenes of Jerry Hawthorn ESQ and
his elegant friend Corinthian Tom in their Rambles and Sprees through
the Metropolis*'. One episode contained a report that Egan had been
unable to supply copy to the printer in time, due to drinking too
much gin (daffy) combined with boiling water at a party at the Albany.
He wrote:

> After a glass or two had been sluiced over the ivories of the
> party, which made some of them loudly to chaff, Bob gave
> the wink to his slavey that more hot water [was] required.
> Large kettle, boiling at the spout provided but instead of
> water, contained boiling daffy. 'Come gents,' said Bob 'please
> yourselves, here's plenty of water, now mix away.'

The drinkers mixed gin with gin and partied until late. Eventually
Egan had to be escorted to his lodgings. While walking somewhat
drunkenly through Leicester Fields, they were 'assailed by some
troublesome customers, and a turn up was the result'.

In another episode, *Taking 'Blue Ruin' at the SLUICERY after
the SPELL is broke up*, Egan describes a typical scene in a gin shop,

highlighting the wide variety of customers it attracts, including gentlemen about town, prostitutes, children and nurses:

JERRY is in Tip Street upon this occasion, and the Mollishers are all nutty upon him, putting it about, one to another, that he is a well-breeched Swell. The left-hand side of the Bar is a 'rich bit' of LOW LIFE; and also points out the depravity of human nature. Gateway PEG has just entered for her ninth glass. This 'lady-bird', who has not only disposed of many an unruly customer in her time, but buzzed them into the bargain, is taking her drops of jackey with OLD MOTHER BRIMSTONE, who has also toddled in to have a flash of lightning before she goes to roost. Both these fair ones (who are as leaky as sieves, from turning their money as fast as they can get it into liquor) are chaffing at 'FAT BET', in consequence to the pretended squeamishness of the latter to TOM, that she had a great objection to every sort of ruin, no matter how it was coloured since she had once queered upon that suit … Mother BRIMSTONE, an old cadger, and a morning-sneak COVESS, who is pouring some blue ruin down the baby's throat to stop its crying, has borrowed the kid in order to assist her in exciting charity from the passing stranger in the street … The Cove and Covess of the Sluicery with faces full of gammon, and who are pocketing the blunt almost as fast they can count it, have just been complaining of the wickedness of the times, and the difficulty of 'paying their way'. SWIPY BILL, a translator of Soles, who has been out for a day's fuddle, for fear his money should become too troublesome to him, has just called in at the gin Spinners to get rid of his last duce by way of a finish, and to have another drop of blue ruin … Kit Blarney, who has just got rid of her sprats, which had been 'up all night' and rather the stronger for the day or two she had had them in her possession, though she had assured her customers all the day they were as fresh as a nosegay, as she had just got them from Billingsgate, has dropped in for the purpose of lighting her short pipe, to get a drap of the CRATURE, and to get rid of the smell of the fish, which remained about her olfactory nerves!

He went on to inform his readers that this scene was nothing unusual: 'The above scene may be nightly witnessed after the SPELL is dissolved, but in much more depraved colours than is here presented. It is, however, LIFE IN LONDON.'

Egan added extra colour to his account by the use of 'Flash', a type of street slang used by the underworld of the period as well as many working-class people. For example, Sluicery is a gin shop, and Gateway Pegg is a prostitute.

Other Victorian slang terms describing gin have entered the English language. Although Jackey, A Flash of Lightning, Blue Ribband, Blue Tape, Lady Dacre's Wine, Rag Water and Strip Me Naked are relatively unknown, Blue Ruin is still frequently used as a brand name for gin. Another nickname, 'daffy', started as a children's medicine, and eventually gained greater currency. Daffy became synonymous with gin, and adults using it were daffiers. An anonymous nineteenth-century verse stated:

> To daffy shops for luscious drops
> Folk stalk in now so numerous,
> And soak their clay with sweet, sweet gin,
> And jest and joke so humorous.

Gin in the workhouse and prison

The frequent availability of gin caused problems in prisons. Writing in the 'State of the Gaols in London', William Smith noted that 120 gallons of gin and 8 butts of beer were drunk at the Kings Bench prison, Southwark every week. This was not just for the gaolers. Prisoners were equally avid drinkers. While inspecting Whitecross Street Prison in London during 1828, Sir Peter Laurie, a magistrate, was informed that a potential steward at the prison had been unsuccessful in his application because the person who took the job sold gin to the prisoners and allowed gambling. This led Laurie to demand that more attention be paid to hunting down the prison's gin suppliers. Codes were often used to identify them, as Mr Pickwick discovered in Charles Dickens' *The Pickwick Papers*, when he heard references to a whistling-shop.

'What is that, Sam? A bird-fancier's?' inquired Mr Pickwick.

'Bless your heart, no, sir. A whistling-shop, sir, is where they sell spirits, a way of prisoners' retailing the favourite article of gin, for their own profit and advantage.'

Officially, gin was not allowed in workhouses unless destined for medicinal use. Workhouse medical officers had a store of liquor for medicinal uses by inmates in the infirmary. At Gressenhall Workshouse, Norfolk, the minutes' books record Best English Gin being purchased at 12s per gallon. Despite this, there were occasions when workhouses experienced problems relating to gin. In 1828, the master of the Aldgate Workhouse appeared in front of the Lord Mayor with his head bandaged. He said it was due to having 'perceived a spirit of insubordination among the paupers', which was due to the provision of gin. A man named Lamb, who acted as a pauper's messenger, was supplying the paupers with gin and had been found carrying seven bottles of gin into the workhouse, despite having been cautioned against such activity on several occasions. When questioned, Lamb claimed that he provided the gin because the inmates needed it saying: 'When they are sick in the bowels, a'nt they to have no-thing to comfort 'em? If they gets a little tossicated, it's because their stomachs is empty.' The Lord Mayor was not convinced and ordered that Lamb should be sent to the House of Correction as a punishment.

Gin palaces

Although gin palaces began to appear in the 1820s, the term did not appear in print until 1833, after which it was used frequently in newspapers and even on the stage. The arrival of gin palaces brought a new dimension into gin retailing; they were very different in appearance to gin shops and created the impression of greater respectability. Distillers like Thompson & Fearon employed prestigious architects, such as John Buonarotti Papworth, to design the gin palaces. Papworth was also responsible for designing the exclusive Boodles gentlemen's club in Mayfair.

Gin palaces were spacious buildings with large windows, often etched with gin brand names and logos. On entering the gin palace, drinkers were greeted by patterned wallpaper, heavy curtains, ornate panelled woodwork, gleaming mahogany bars and gas lighting. Writer Henry Vizetelly noted:

> It was near Field Lane that the first London gin palace was built. The polished mahogany counters, the garish bar fittings, the smartly painted vats, inscribed 'Old Tom' and 'Cream of the Valley' the rows of showy bottles of noyau and other cordials, and above all the immense blaze of gas light within and without these buildings as soon as dusk set in, were all so many novelties and came as a vision of splendour to the besotted denizens of the neighbouring slums.

George Wilson of Tothill Street, Westminster complained to a parliamentary select committee on drunkenness that a 'low dirty public house' just across the road from his business had been transformed into a gin palace. He stated that it was:

> A splendid edifice, the front ornamental with pilasters, supporting a handsome cornice and entablature and balustrades, and the whole elevation remarkably striking and handsome ... the doors and windows glazed with very large squares of plate glass, and the gas fittings of the most costly description ... When this edifice was completed, note was given by placards taken around the parish, a band of music was stationed in front ... The street became almost impassable from the number of people collected; and when the doors were opened, the rush was tremendous, it was instantly filled with customers, and continued so till midnight.

The gin palaces undoubtedly attracted attention. A Temperance campaigner recorded seeing a gin palace possessing 'no less than THREE enormous lamps with corresponding lights', while another 'had a revolving light with many burners playing most beautifully over the door'. Such scenes would have created a beacon of light in the dimly lit streets. The costs of creating a gin palace were high, with some contemporary estimates suggested that it could be as much as £3,000. The Temperance Movement reckoned it could cost £2,000 for a simple gin palace with the most impressive and palatial building costing £10,000.

Writing in *Sketches by Boz*, Dickens commented:

> Ingenuity is exhausted in devising attractive titles for the different descriptions of gin; and the dram-drinking portion of the community as they gaze upon the gigantic black and white announcements, which are only to be equalled in size by the figures beneath them, are left in a state of pleasing

hesitation between 'The Cream of the Valley', 'the Out and Out', 'The No Mistake', 'The Good for mixing', 'The real Knock-me-down', 'The celebrated Butter Gin', 'The regular Flare-up'. ... The Gin-shops in and near Drury Lane, Holborn, St Giles's, Covent Garden and Clare-market, are the handsomest in London...

He pointed out that such premises contrasted dramatically with their setting as 'There is more of filth and squalid misery near those great thorough-fares than in any part of this mighty city.' Merely turning the corner from the Rookery near Drury Lane, complete with 'wretched houses with broken windows patched with rags and paper, every room let out to a different family...filth everywhere...men and women, in every variety of scanty and dirty apparel, lounging, scolding, drinking, smoking, squabbling, fighting, and swearing' marked a dramatic difference.

Dickens went on to write:

You turn the corner ... All is light and brilliancy. The hum of many voices issues from that splendid gin-shop which forms the commencement of the two streets opposite; and the gay building with the fantastically ornamented parapet, the illuminated clock, the plate-glass windows surrounded by stucco rosettes, and its profusion of gas-lights in richly-gilt burners, is perfectly dazzling when contrasted with the darkness and dirt we have just left.

Inside, the gin was sold neat, infused and with water. One of the most popular versions was Cream Gin, made by infusing gin with cream and sugar in the barrel. Each barrel was emblazed with an appropriate name, such as Cream of the Valley, Best Cordial Gin, Butter Gin, or the Knock Me Down. Dickens noted the existence of 'two side-aisle of great casks, painted green and gold, enclosed with a tight brass rail and bearing such descriptions as 'Old Tom 549' and 'Young Tom 360', 'Samson 1421'. On the counter were, 'in addition to the usual spirit apparatus, two or three little baskets of cakes and biscuits, which are carefully secured at top with wicker-work, to prevent their contents being unlawfully abstracted.' Serving the customers' requests for spirits and compounds were 'two showily-dressed damsels with large necklaces' and 'the ostensible proprietor of the concern, a stout, coarse fellow in a fur cap, put on very much on one side to give him a knowing air, and to display his sandy whiskers to the best advantage.'

Testifying to the parliamentary committee on drunkenness in 1834, George Wilson was dismissive when it came to considering staffing conditions at a gin palace. He commented men worked 'in their shirt sleeves behind the counters, the exertion from the number of customers not allowing them to wear their coats'. Even after the heyday of the gin palace, staff worked extremely hard. In 1859, journalist George Augustus Sala reported observing a barman in constant motion, 'one hand on a tap, the other presented for the requisite halfpence … His face is flushed; his manner short, concise, sententious. His vocabulary is limited; a short "Now then", and a brief "Here you are", forming the staple phrases thereof.'

Customers were not encouraged to stay long. They purchased their drink, emptied their glass and left quickly by a different door. Theodore Sedgwick II, an American lawyer visiting London in 1836 and exploring the world of gin palaces around Holborn, noted that men, women and children went in one door and out another. He wrote that no one stayed long as 'they came in, drank and went off.' Thomson & Fearon claimed that 8 out of 10 customers spent less than a minute drinking their gin before leaving. In the mid-1830s, Temperance Society members observing a Manchester gin palace popular with factory workers noted it was frequented by 'not fewer than 2,000 persons, chiefly females' on a Saturday night, while another served an average of 163 women and 112 men every 40 minutes. He also came to the conclusion that the gin served was 'undoubtedly adulterated; it seemed to be sweetened, and certainly had not the flavour of pure gin'.

The speed at which customers were served explains why sales were so high. The fourteen largest gin palaces in London were known to be able to serve half a million customers every week. With no seating provided, customers were not able to sit down and relax, or discuss business. A visit to a gin palace was purely for a quick, fast drink. Maximising sales was crucial. Different types of customers entered by different doors, such as a jug and bottle entrance for customers wanting gin to take out, a retail bar for a quick drink, and a wholesale entrance for customers buying large quantities.

Children were frequently seen in the gin palaces. George Cruikshank's 1839 engraving of *The Gin Shop* in *Sketches by Boz* shows a little boy standing at the counter, waiting to be served with gin. Thomas Miller noted again:

> Women, and children even, are coming in with bottles; some of the latter so little, that, like the one which our artist has so truthfully sketched, they are scarcely able to reach up and place the bottle upon the zinc-covered bar. If the weather is cold they are generally sent out in their mothers' shawls and bonnets, the one trailing upon the ground, and the other completely burying their little dirty faces. Even these young miserable creatures are fond of drink, and may sometimes be seen slily drawing the cork outside the door, and lifting the poisonous potion to their white withered lips. They have already found that gin numbs and destroys for a time the gnawing pangs of hunger, and they can drink the fiery mixture in its raw state.

Fast turnover of drinkers was undoubtedly the key element in the activities of gin palaces, but as *The London Journal of Flora Tristan 1803–1844* indicates, some of the establishments had an extra function. Flora Tristan was an aristocrat and feminist linked to a prominent

Peruvian family who visited England and explored London. She describes watching the activities of prostitutes in the West End, and later seeing them in a gin palace. Beginning their day with attempts to gain customers while walking in the West End, they steadily descend further and further through society as the day progresses, ending in the 'finishes' which are 'vast, sumptuous taverns where one goes to finish out the night'.

She continues:

> These splendid taverns have a very special character. It seems that their frequenters are dedicated to the night; they go to bed when the sun begins to light up the horizon, and they get up after it has gone down. On the outside these carefully shut-up palace-taverns betoken only sleep and silence; but the porter has hardly opened the little door where the initiates enter than one is dazzled by the lively, brilliant lights escaping from a thousand gas jets. On the second floor there is an immense salon divided into two parts lengthwise. In the one part is a row of tables separated by wooden partitions, as in all the English restaurants. On two sides of the tables are sofa-benches. Opposite on the other side of the room, is a stage where richly costumed prostitutes are on display.
>
> Toward midnight the habitués begin to arrive. Several of these taverns are the meeting places for high society where the elite of the aristocracy assembles. ... The orgy is steadily rising to a crescendo, between four and five o'clock in the morning it reaches its peak.

In 1875, James Greenwood described 'A Night with Old Tom' where he viewed

> the miserable ones who are afflicted with this insatiable gin-hunger, possessing the stealthy, oft-repeated 'dram' in the vain

hope to quench the impotent thirst for gin which consumes them. It is not for such as these that the gas and glitter, the plate-glass and the flashy emblazonment of ceilings and panels has attractions ... The only place where they would pledge 'the cup of friendship' – if they owned such an article representing value – would be at the pawnbrokers. To linger over their libations is to them a tantalization – a weariness and a waste of time. If they could anyhow contrive it, they would get drink at a leap as it were, and have done with it. ... He has the money all ready in his hand and catching the barmaid's eye he ejaculates as hurriedly as though he had not a moment to spare, 'Glass of Old Tom'. In seven seconds the liquor is drawn, the vessel raised to his pale lean jaws, and with a sudden gulp, such as ordinarily attends the swallowing of a pill, it is gone.

Writing in the *Illustrated London News* in 1848, Thomas Miller described the typical gin palace customers. In an article entitled 'The Dram Drinker' he states:

There are few places in London where so great a variety of characters may be seen popping and out in a short space of time, as in the bars of our modern-gin palaces. Even respectable men who meet each other by chance, must drop in the nearest tavern, although they have scarcely a minute to spare, to drink a glass together at the bar, and enquire about old friends. Married women ... also congregate when they ought to be providing the dinner for their families. ... Then there are the young itinerant vendors of almost every imaginable thing – these are, also, constant members of the bar, confining themselves generally to pennyworths of gin. The costermongers, who come wheeling and shouting from opposite directions, with their barrows, if they chance to meet near the door of a tavern must, after a little gossip, go in and have their 'dram'. Added to these, there are the poor, the old and the miserable, who look and feel 'half-dead' as they themselves express it, unless they are 'lighted up' every two or three hours with a glass of spirits ... the 'palace' is always crowded with guests who, standing, staggering, crouching, or lying down, groaning, and cursing, drink and forget.

Originating in London, the concept of gin palaces quickly spread nationwide, catering particularly for the ever-growing numbers of industrial workers employed in manufacturing facilities. Writing in *History Today* 'Gin in Regency England' (March 2011), historian Jessica Warner points out that 'gin palaces began to appear in all of England's rapidly growing towns and cities – in Manchester and its suburbs of Bolton and Blackburn, in Birmingham, Leeds, Liverpool and Hull – but also in smaller places such as Lincoln and Scarborough.'

It was a profitable business both for the distillers and the gin palace owners. Most lived as far as possible away from their trading premises, or if they did live on site, spent little time with their customers. David Brooke, a Leeds factory worker, told the parliamentary committee on drunkenness that the owner of a gin palace in Leeds had moved into a new house in the suburbs, which was 'more like a mansion than a tradesman's residence'. George Wilson made a similar criticism referring to landlords who lived like gentlemen and kept 'horses and grooms, and large establishments, and shopmen to serve their customers', regarding their main working function as being to 'superintend the counting-house department, and give orders to those around them'. In 1838, the *Morning Chronicle* referred to the 'gin-seller, who drives up to his establishment in his four-wheel chaise, and who leaves the spinning of his gin and the gathering of his large profits to his barmaids'.

Accusations of improper business practices were common, as observers sought to understand exactly how the gin palaces generated a high turnover. Henry Winchester, Lord Mayor of London, commented in 1834 that 'either the gin must be very bad, or the glasses very small, to afford any profit'. There were reports that in some establishments, glasses were designed to hold just a farthing's worth of gin, while in Manchester there were rumours of 'squib' glasses being used. These 'squib' glasses held gin worth halfpence and were designed for Manchester's child labourers.

The arrival of gin palaces worried publicans. The Association of Licensed Victuallers complained that gin palaces encouraged immorality, and threatened that 'they would be compelled in self-defence to convert their houses into gin palaces, and pull down the parlours and taprooms provided for the accommodation of travellers and labourers.' Gin shops and gin palaces were quite simply more attractive to working-class people because they provided drink at an affordable price. Pubs were more expensive, and sought a more affluent clientele, such as travellers seeking overnight accommodation, or people wanting a meal as well as a drink, rather than ordinary working-class people. In 1826, writer Sydney Smith pointed out that pubs were 'treating humble and ill-dressed people with the most sovereign contumely and contempt'.

It was not just publicans who were concerned. In 1829, the Middlesex magistrates, responsible for licensing pubs throughout north London, recommended withholding licences from speculators who were seeking to buy out alehouses and turn them into gin palaces retailing spirits.

It was only when Parliament finally took action that the number of gin shops and gin palaces began to decline. In the 1830 Beer Act, Parliament removed the duty payable on British beer thus immediately making it less expensive to purchase. Any ratepayer was able to sell it to the public on purchase of a licence costing just 2 guineas. This made it more economical to sell beer to all classes of society in comfortable surroundings, accompanied by food and seating. Within six months, over 25,000 such licences had been granted. At the same time, publicans utilised lessons learned from the gin palaces – pubs were increasingly made more comfortable and far less dingy than had previously been the practice. The pubs were also more sociable, providing a place to chat and enjoy a variety of pub games such as skittles and quoits. Pubs and gin palaces eventually became almost indistinguishable. The Viaduct Tavern in Newgate Street, London is one of the original Victorian gin palaces, built in 1869. The interior still includes a traditional gin booth and has an extensive gin menu. Likewise, the countless gin bars that have opened around the country since the millennium now sell both gin and beer, thus attracting a varied clientele.

Gin in Victorian literature and art

By the mid-nineteenth century, the advent of high quality distillers was beginning to make gin a much more respectable drink, which was accepted at all levels of society. Prominent people began to visit gin palaces or were known to be drinking gin in their homes. It also featured in the literature and art of the period. Yet despite this increasing social acceptability, the gin industry still attracted criticism due to the problems of alcoholism.

Novelist Charles Dickens was a keen gin drinker. He drank gin and water at Jack Straw's Castle or the Spaniards Inn when walking on Hampstead Heath, frequently ordered a Summer Gin Punch at the Garrick Club, and served Gin Slings to his guests at his Gad's Hill home.

Charles Lamb, author of countless poems and plays as well as the best-selling children's *Tales from Shakespeare*, was another enthusiastic gin drinker, becoming addicted to it even though he was aware of the dangers. Writing in his book *Confessions* he stated, 'the drinking man is never less himself than during his sober intervals' and although he tried to abstain from what he described as the 'poisonous potion', it caused him to 'scream out, to cry aloud, for the anguish and pain within him'.

Despite this greater respectability, questions continued to arise concerning the quality of the beverage being supplied. In May 1868, Charles Dickens wrote to the Millbank Distillery expressing concern about a recent delivery of gin:

> Mr Charles Dickens sends his compliments to Messrs. Seager Evans and Co. and begs them to test the accompanying bottle of gin drawn from their cask this morning. It appears to Mr Dickens to have neither the right strength nor flavour, and he thinks it must have been tampered with at the Railway. When the cask was tapped at Gad's Hill on Saturday, it was observed to be particularly full.

In the *Boozing Ken Once More* by George Reynolds, adulteration becomes a topic of conversation among drinkers.

> 'What have you got to say agin blue ruin, old feller?' demanded a Knacker, who was regaling himself with a glass of gin-and-water.

> 'Blue ruin – gin!' cried the old man. 'Ah! I can tell you something about that too. Oil of vitriol is the chief ingredient: it has the pungency and smell of gin. When you take the cork out of a bottle of pure gin, it will never make your eyes water: but the oil of vitriol will. Ha! Ha! There's a test for you. Try it! Oil of turpentine, sulphuric ether, and oil of almonds are used to conceal the vitriol in the made–up gin. What is called Fine Cordial Gin is the most adulterated of all: it is concocted expressly for dram–drinkers – ha! Ha!'

Writing in *The Curious Bartenders Gin Palace*, Tristan Stephenson points out that *Adulterated Detected*, an 1847 manual on how to detect fraudulent spirit, compares recipes for both London and

Plymouth gins, where the recipe for 'Plain or London Gin' includes '700 gallons of the second rectification, 70lbs German juniper berries, 70lbs coriander seeds, 3.5lbs almond cake, 1.5lbs angelica root, 6lbs liquorice powder', whereas 'West Country Gin, known as Plymouth Gin' is made from the same quantity of spirit and only '14lbs German juniper berries, 1.5lbs clamus root and 8lbs sulphuric acid.'

Examples of adulteration continued to arise. In 1877, the Local Government Board claimed that 50 per cent of gin contained copper to heighten the colour and give it a 'glow'.

Gin punch was a popular option at events at all levels of society. The 1827 Oxford Nightcaps pamphlet commissioned by Oxford University contains a recipe for gin punch made using 2 pints of gin, oranges, lemons, capillaire (a form of sugar syrup) calves foot jelly and white wine. Four years later, the exclusive Garrick Club in London used a gin punch recipe involving 'half a pint of gin, lemon peel, lemon juice, sugar, maraschino, a pint and quarter of water, and two bottles of iced soda water.' Bob Cratchit, the poverty-stricken clerk in Charles Dickens' *A Christmas Carol*, created a festive drink for his family: 'Turning up his cuffs, – as if, poor fellow, they were capable of being made any more shabby – compounded some hot mixture in a jug with gin and lemons and stirred it round and round and put it on the hob to simmer.'

In Charles Dickens' *Bleak House*, links between drunkenness and a disreputable underclass are stressed with his description of Mr Krook, a rag and bone merchant who lives on gin. A bottle of gin has a permanent place on his table.

For illustrators the evils of gin drinking and alcoholism provided considerable inspiration as the images that could be created were intensely memorable. The message being created Charles Jameson Grant's 1834 image *The Drunkards Progress* could not be more obvious. It shows a line of poverty-stricken men, women and children lined up from a money lender's shop to the 'Temple of Juniper: Best Gin'. In the background there are crowds of poor people in the doorways of the gaol and workhouse. The caption points out that the path of gin led 'from the Pawnbroker's to the Gin Shop, from thence to the Workhouse, thence to the Gaol and ultimately to the Scaffold'.

Yet another drawing from the same year by Grant entitled *A gin palace as a 'temple of Juniper'* illustrates a gentleman giving a piece of paper to a poverty-stricken family, even as other impoverished people stumble around or collapse on the floor. One woman holds a bottle of gin while her child lies dead beside her. Numerous other men wearing bowler hats converse in a grim fashion as pieces of paper are exchanged between them. Gin salesmen reminiscent of quack doctors promise all kinds of benefits to their customers. Barrels surround the room bearing statues referring to the effects of gin: poverty, despair, disease, insanity, blasphemy, plunder, murder and death. Two bodies hang above a statue entitled 'delusion inviting her victims in'.

Cruikshank was one of the most prolific such illustrators, and was himself a former heavy drinker who had become a follower of the Temperance Movement in the 1840s. In 1868, he published an image, *The Gin Shop,* which showed a man and woman talking with two children. The woman is pointing to a sign in a shop highlighting Christmas Gin, even as a man in torn clothes walks past – a reminder of the evils of drink. A wood engraving entitled *The Clew* by Charles Keene published in *Punch* in 1879, showed a street scene involving a sobbing child. The accompanying caption read:

> The child was evidently lost! – cried bitterly – could not tell where its Parents lived, or whether she was an Orphan, or what her Father was – or where she went to School. – Enter Intelligent Policeman.
>
> Policeman (in a friendly whisper), 'Where does your Mother get her Gin, My Dear?'

[And the mystery was solved.]

Chapter 5

The Deadly Drink

Gin can be deadly, as people have discovered all too often. Across the centuries, adulteration has caused serious illnesses and even death. The distilling process itself has caused numerous problems, resulting in explosions and serious injury. It has been linked to murders and crimes, as well as the problems caused by alcoholism arising from excessive gin drinking.

Gin and crime

During the 1700s, over 1,120 court cases at London's Old Bailey involved crimes in which gin played a prominent role. Gin shops were notorious for being the meeting places of outlaws, thieves and the receivers of stolen goods. Outlaw Dick Turpin was often seen drinking in the gin shops around London's East End. The London Grand Jury noted, 'Most of the Murders and Robberies lately committed have been laid and concentrated at Gin Shops' adding that 'fired with these Hot Spirits' criminals 'prepared to execute the most bold and daring Attempts'. Henry Fielding, chief magistrate at Bow Street commented: 'I have plainly perceived, from the State of the Case, that the Gin alone was the cause of the transgression, and have been sometimes sorry that I was obliged to commit them to Prison.'

The practice of publishing last confessions from convicted prisoners at Newgate Gaol, London clearly revealed numerous links to gin, blaming it for their predicament. In February 1728, Joseph Barret, a 42-year-old labourer, was found guilty of killing his 11-year-old son James. His last confession noted that he and his wife had become more and more concerned about his son's activities because he was 'Night after Night coming home in the greatest Disorder imaginable' and that 'he beg'd Money from People and brought Gin with it, drinking till he appear'd worse than a Beast, quite out of his Senses'. Faced with this situation, Barret decided to take action. Having previously served in the Royal Navy, Barret 'prepared a Cat of Nine-Tails for his Chastisement' but had 'no evil intention … only to reclaim him (if possible) from his wild Courses'. Unfortunately the beating was so ferocious that James took to his bed and died. Joseph Barret was convicted of murder and hung on the gallows. He shared the scaffold with a 22-year-old burglar named George Weeden, whose last confession indicated Weeden had turned to crime because of gin, having met a gang of thieves in a gin shop. Some years later, 20-year-old James Baker met the same fate, describing himself as 'one of them who frequented Gin-shops' and 'got into the acquaintance of the vilest Company in the World, who for two or three Years past, drove him headlong to destruction and into all kinds of Villanies.'

By far the most notorious eighteenth-century thief was Jack Sheppard. Born into a poor family, he was apprenticed as a carpenter in London before taking up a different career: that of theft and burglary. He was arrested and imprisoned five times in 1724, but escaped on four occasions, gaining considerable notoriety as a result. After his escapes, he was frequently to be found drinking gin and eating oysters in Drury Lane taverns rather than fleeing from the area.

In 1724, he wrote an account of one of his escapes saying:

> after fileing, Defileing, Sawing, Climbing' to freedom out of condemned cell Newgate' … went on to Shoe-Lane but there meeting with a Bully Hack of the Town, he would have shov'd me down, which my Spirit resenting, though a brawny Dog, I soon Coller'd him, fell Souse at him, then with his own Cane I strappe'd till he was forced to Buckle too, and hold his Tongue … and was glad to pack off at Last and turn his

heels upon me ... and dextrously made a Hand of my Feet
under the Leg-Tavern ... By this time being Fainty and nigh
Spent, I put forward and seeing a Light near the Savoy-Gate,
I was resolved not to make Light of the Opportunity, but
call'd for a hearty Dram of Luther and Calvin, that is, Mum
(beer) and Geneva mix'd, but having Fasted so long before, it
soon got into my Noddle, and o-er I had gone twenty steps, it
had so entirely Stranded my Reason, that by the time I came
to Half-Moon-Street end, it gave a New-Exchange to my
senses, and made me quite Lunatick.

On the occasion of his final arrest he was reported to be blind drunk.
On the eve of his execution, he had a drinking match with Figg the
prize fighter, with yet more drink being enjoyed en route to the gallows.

Joseph Dalton was another seventeenth-century, gin-loving thief.
Having been convicted of theft, he was sentenced to transportation to
America. The journey did not go according to plan, with subsequent
reports being made that:

one Hescot [a fellow prisoner of Dalton], a Prisoner, who
had about fifty pound o Bisket, two Caggs of Genever, a
Cheese and some Butter on board, when up one day upon
Deck for the Air ... we ransacked all his Stores; but upon
his Return, he finding out what had been done, went and
made Complaint to the Captain, who threaten'd to whip
us all round to find out the right Man, whereupon sixteen
of us agreed to secure the whole Ship's crew (being but
twelve in Number, Captain and Boy included) before the
Whipping Gale blew harder ... once in control, shared out
Hescot's Genever, agreed that everyone that was drunk
upon his Watch, so as his Arms could be taken from him, or
was caught in the hold with the Women Prisoners, should
receive twelve lashes.

The story goes that Dalton and his fellow mutineers then drank a final toast of genever with the captain and his mate, before being put ashore at Cape Finisterre. Dalton eventually headed back to London, where he was caught and executed.

Felons on the way to the gallows were frequently allowed to stop off at gin shops along the route, as well as being given more gin to drink at the very last minute. It was not unknown for the hangman also to be drunk on arrival at the gallows, and there are instances where the hangman tried to hang the priest giving the convicted felon the last rites.

Gin was equally essential for those involved in laying out the dead, as Dickens points out in *Martin Chuzzlewit*. Mrs Gamp is permanently surrounded with a 'smell of spirits' and comments: 'if it wasn't for the nerve a little sip of liquor gives me … I never could go through with what I sometimes has to do.' Dickens is said to have based her character on a real nurse that he had encountered.

By the early 1800s, it was known that excessive drinking could cause hallucinations. Gin was said to cause 'terrible hangovers, depression or even insanity'.

The story of Thomas Bedworth is a good example. Bedworth was executed in 1815 for the murder of his lover, Elisabeth Beesmore. Both had already experienced failed marriages, and they began a bigamous relationship, which became increasingly acrimonious. Then Elisabeth's husband reappeared, forcing Bedworth to move out of their joint lodgings. Saying he would kill her, Bedworth sought refuge in drink, becoming almost constantly drunk. On the day of the murder, everyone involved, including Elisabeth, was drinking gin in various gin shops. Drunk, Bedworth returned to Elisabeth's room carrying a sharp, shoemaker's knife. As she was not in her room, he promptly went back to the gin shop for another drink. He was extremely drunk by the time he eventually met Elisabeth, and she allowed him to stay and sleep it off. On waking, he left the room minus his shoes and coat, and purchased more gin. On his return, Elisabeth gave him tea laced with gin. Just before he left again, he called her into the kitchen and they embraced. Caught by 'jealous passion and strong affection', Bedworth drew his knife and slashed her throat. Still extremely drunk, he walked to Regent's Park where he threw his knife into the canal, and went into hiding.

Remaining totally intoxicated, he spent the next few nights hearing her voice saying, 'O Bedworth! Bedworth! What have you done? You have deprived me of all the happiness of this life', along with the constant sound of agonising moans. At one point, he walked up Highgate Hill only to see her ghost in front of him, then it moved to walk beside him and took his hand placing it on her severed throat. Fleeing in terror, he collapsed in a field where her ghost lay down beside him. Almost insane with fear, he resolved to leave London and despite having an arrest warrant issued against him, he managed to obtain a Walking Pass allowing him to travel. He eventually ended up in Coventry where the haunting came to a temporary end – only to start again a short time later. Unable to take any more, Bedworth turned himself in at a local police station where he was arrested and taken back to London. In his written confession, he claimed that his passion had been inflamed by drink. The judge gave a verdict of wilful murder and sentenced him to the gallows, with his body being sent to the surgeons for dissection.

It is believed that drinking excessive amounts of gin was a cause of the murder, while the withdrawal from drink afterwards may well have caused him to believe he was seeing her ghost. Bedworth would have been suffering from delirium tremens due to the sudden change in his drinking habits. 'Nightmares, confusion, disorientation, visual and auditory hallucinations, tactile hallucinations' are among the main side effects of the condition.

Among the most notorious of all murders linked to gin are those of Jack the Ripper, the Victorian serial killer operating in the East End of London in 1888. Several of the victims were described as being gin drinkers. For example, Liz Stride was said to have spent all night before her death drinking gin. Some reports suggest that Catherine Eddowes was so drunk on gin that she was taken into police custody for her own safety. After she sobered up, she was released only to seek more drink and became a victim of Jack the Ripper. Other gin connections included references to a 'ginny kidney' initially believed to have come from Catherine because she was a heavy drinker. It was later accepted that the kidney was not from her body, and had just been preserved in gin. Reports suggest that it was the result of a medical student playing a prank.

In 1891, Mr Montagu Williams, a magistrate from the Worship Street Police Court in London, told *The Strand* magazine that from his experience, drink was the cause of nearly all the crime in London's East End and that 'wives were often worse than husbands … the woman often makes the first start towards breaking up the home whilst the husband is away at work. She forsakes her children and domestic cares for the bar of a gin shop to drink with a friend, generally another woman.'

Officials and society at large tended to regard a woman drinker as being unsavoury, a poor mother and wife. As a result, there were occasions when murderers and criminals sought to use this as an excuse for their actions. A typical example is that of Matthias Brinsden who was charged with murdering his wife, Hannah, by stabbing her in the chest at their home within the parish of St Ann Blackfriars, near St Paul's Cathedral. At his trial, in order gain sympathy from the jurors and magistrate, he claimed she suffered from a gin addiction. Brinsden claimed that he reached for a knife because Hannah was 'half speed' (drunk) and wanted to join her friends at the gin shop and sought to leave the house unobserved. When he saw her going to the door, he 'turn'd about with the Knife in his Hand, to prevent her, and she in Strugling to get out, thrust herself against it before he was aware.' His argument was not accepted and he was found guilty of murder. Character witnesses were called to prove that he was known to be a 'very ill husband, often abusing and beating his wife'. Other witnesses proved that he had stabbed Hannah because she asked him for meat for supper, which he could not provide.

The links between gin and crime have persisted. The Kray Brothers were a prominent 1960s' East London crime gang, involved in extremely violent attacks. Their favourite tipple was a gin and tonic. Reggie Kray tended to live in a gin-soaked alcoholic haze, often drinking a bottle of gin every night. He used to drink in the Blind Beggar pub in Whitechapel, accompanied by his brother, Ronnie. The duo were involved in the brutal murder of Jack 'The Hat' McVitie before spending many years in prison. Subsequent films such as *The Krays* (1990) and *Legend* (2015) have glamorised the ambiance of smoky pubs inhabited by gin-fuelled villains.

The adulteration of gin

Gin adulteration was a major problem during the eighteenth and nineteenth centuries, when noxious substances hazardous to health, such as turpentine, were often added to the liquid. Although adulteration is now rare, there are occasional examples of this practice still occurring.

In 2014, backpacker Cheznye Emmons from Essex died after drinking adulterated gin while on holiday in Indonesia. She and her boyfriend had purchased a bottle of gin from a shop in Bukit Lawang, Northern Sumatra. The label on the bottle appeared legitimate, but in reality it contained fake gin laced with methanol, a substance that is usually transformed into formaldehyde. Just 10ml of methanol can cause permanent blindness. After drinking the gin, Cheznye went blind, suffered convulsions and died in hospital five days later. Police investigating her death discovered a warehouse where over 5,000 bottles of the fake gin were stored. Even after her death, some of the bottles could still be found on sale in stores around Bukit Lawang.

A further example of adulteration came to light in Manila, Philippines in 2019. Complaints were made about a poisonous gin known as Cosmic Carabao, distributed by Juan Brew Inc.

The investigations began after women vomited or fainted after drinking the gin, and had to be taken to hospital. One of the victims had suffered from methanol poisoning. All the Cosmic Carabao products were immediately recalled.

Similar incidents have occurred in Nigeria. Adulterated gin caused the death of a 16-year-old boy who couldn't resist the temptation of drinking some of the extra gin he had been given to take home by a local supplier. He went into convulsions and died in hospital. Elsewhere in Nigeria, a brand called Ogogoro Gin was impounded in Warri in July 2020, because it had been adulterated with methanol.

An earlier instance of adulteration took place in 2015, when David Ozoemenam was arrested in Lagos for supplying adulterated gin. Investigators discovered vast quantities of empty bottles within his house, together with fake labels and brands carrying National Agency for Food and Drug Administration and Control (NAFDAC) names and numbers. He told investigators that he saw nothing wrong with the practice:

> My brand name is Stock and I manufacture Stock Gins and Brandy. I don't have a NAFDAC number because at the time I started, I had financial problems and I could not pay for a NAFDAC number. Customers don't know the difference between a genuine and a fake NAFDAC number, they feel it is a waste of time to check it. The majority of the customers don't have time to examine the number pasted on the bottles.

When asked if his products might pose a health hazard, he responded, 'There is no health hazard because I used to taste it before I supplied to customers.'

Combustible gin

Even the production of gin can be deadly. The distilling process involves the use of combustible substances. The copper stills used to distil gin have been known to explode, causing severe injury. In Texas, USA, an explosion caused by a butane gas leak at the Flower Grove Co-Op Gin led to the destruction of the entire interior of the building. Three employees were hospitalised and the distillery lost over a year's production. Likewise in the UK, an explosion at Langley's Distillery, Oldbury sent flames shooting 50 feet into the air, with lamp posts and window frames in nearby streets melting. Over 200 people had to be evacuated from their homes, and 16 houses were left uninhabitable.

Dark connotations

Gin has aroused more controversy over the centuries than any other form of alcohol. A disreputable history of social turmoil, mass drunkenness and frequent adulteration has evolved into emotive advertising, often arousing considerable controversy. Distillers have taken the dark images and dark connotations accrued by gin throughout its history and combined them with folklore and legends to develop memorable branding. Even chefs like Heston Blumenthal have utilised the dark connotations of gin to create unusual experiences.

Gin has also generated countless nicknames – mostly female orientated. This is mainly due to the fact that women have often been perceived to be falling foul of gin more frequently than men, and links with abortions have not helped. Names like Madame Geneva (a corruption of the Dutch name for gin), Ladies' Delight and Mother Gin became commonplace, as did less salubrious ones like Mother's Ruin, Jenny Pisspot and Dorothy Addlebrain.

The problems of alcoholism

The eighteenth-century Gin Craze created an awareness of the problems of alcoholism, an awareness which had not previously existed. Although getting drunk on various alcoholic liquids was nothing new, it had never before affected entire populations of an area.

Contemporary observers wrote accounts of dreadful scenes involving drunken people in the streets placing the blame firmly on gin.

Writing in his political study of 1714, *The Fable of the Bees: or, Private Vices, Publick Benefits*, Anglo–Dutch philosopher Bernard Mandeville noted that although drinking gin caused problems at home due to alcohol abuse, it acted as a boost to morale and helped motivate soldiers and sailors to greater efforts during combat. He wrote:

> whatever sloth and sottishness might be caused by the abuse of malt spirit, the moderate use of it was of inestimable benefit to the poor, who could not afford cordials at higher prices … the losses we suffered from the insignificant quarrels alcohol created at home were thoroughly outweighed by the advantage we received from it abroad, by upholding the courage of soldiers and animating the sailors to the combat; and that in the last two wars every considerable victory was obtained with help from alcohol.

> … Nothing is more destructive, either in regard to the health or the vigilance and industry of the poor, than the infamous liquor, the name of which, derived from Juniper, in Dutch … shrunk to a monosyllable, intoxicating Gin.

Gin is seen as the cause of numerous 'maladies' and has become a 'liquid poison' due to its destructive qualities. Mandeville goes on to state that gin

> charms the unactive, the desperate and crazy of either sex, and makes the starving sot behold his rags and nakedness with stupid indolence. It is a fiery lake that sets the brain in flame, burns up the entrails, and scorches every part within; and at the same time, a Lethe of oblivion, in which the wretch immersed drowns.

He concludes by stating that gin has 'broke and destroy'd the strongest Constitutions, thrown 'em into Consumptions, and been the fatal and immediate occasion of Apoplexies, Phrensies and sudden Death.'

Increasing attention was also being paid to the effects of excessive drinking on the body, and on future generations. Daniel Defoe wrote in 1728 that excessive gin drinking would mean 'in less than an Age, we may expect a fine Spindle-shank'd Generation'. A similar view was taken by the Grand Jury to the City of London which noted that gin was making 'our lower Kind of People … enfeebled and disabled, having neither the Will nor Powere to Labour for an honest Livelihood'.

In 1751, the *London Magazine, or Gentleman's Monthly Intelligencer* contained a sarcastic suggestion for a gin bottle label:

When fam'd Pandora to the cloud withdrew,
From her dire box unnumber'd evils flew,
No less a curse this vehicle contains;-
Fire to the mind, and poison to the vein.

The implication was obvious – just like Pandora's Box, once opened the bottle releases countless evils that cannot easily be recalled. The same year, Josiah Tucker wrote that gin's greatest crime was the fact that it needed so little time to disturb the brain and make it subject to delusions: 'instantaneous Drunkenness where a man hat no time to recollect or think, whether he had had enough or not … smallness of the quantity deceives him so that his reason is gone before he is aware' becoming 'mad and furious, without Sense or Duty, Fear or Shame'.

Three years later, Stephen Hales wrote in *A friendly Admonition to Drinkers of Gin, Brandy etc.,* 'that experiments in which alcoholic spirits had been fed directly into the veins of animals revealed that spirits like gin often caused "Obstructions and Stoppages in the Liver" resulting in jaundice, Dropsy, and many other fatal Diseases.'

He went on to say that spirits 'destroy and burn up the Lungs', and 'weaken and wear out the Substance and Coats of the Stomach'. In order to recover from this, drinkers need to be 'dealt like a Madman, and be bound down to keep him from destroying himself'. Hales believed that sufferers could be weaned off drink by providing increasingly diluted spirits over the period of a week.

Physicians began to research the problem, altering their viewpoint from regarding drunkenness as just a sin to seeing it as a medical condition. Erasmus Darwin recognised his first wife, Mary, was addicted to wine and gin. She died aged 31, probably from cirrhosis of the liver. As a result of this experience, Darwin began to argue that liver cancer arose from alcohol abuse. Although he accepted the prevailing view that alcoholism was hereditary, he believed that it could be overcome by willpower, just like seasickness.

In 1804, another physician, Thomas Trotter, wrote *An Essay, Medical, Philosophical, and Chemical, on Drunkenness and its effects on the Human Body*, stating that 'the habit of drunkenness is a disease of the mind' and that it was not just physical but also emotional. He advocated counselling and improving a person's self-esteem, as well as seeking to decrease their alcohol consumption.

Dickens went further still by pointing out that social issues could make alcohol problems worse. He wrote in *Sketches by Boz:*

> Gin drinking is a great vice in England, but wretchedness and dirt are greater; and until you improve the homes of the poor, or persuade a half-famished wretch not to seek relief in the temporary oblivion of his own misery, with the pittance which, divided among his family, would furnish a morsel of bread for each, gin shops will increase in number and splendour.

Observations of excessive gin consumption also led to greater understanding as to why alcoholics often had a blue tinge to their skin. In 1888, the social observer Walter Besant noted:

Some time ago, I saw, going into a public house, somewhere near the West India Docks, a tall lean man, apparently five-and-forty or thereabouts. He was in rags, his knees bent as he walked, his hands trembled, his eyes were eager. And wonderful to relate, the face was perfectly blue – not indigo blue, or azure blue, but of a ghostly, ghastly, corpse-like kind of blue, which made one shudder. Said my companion to me, 'That is gin.' We opened the door of the public house and looked in. He stood at the bar with a full glass in his hand. Then his eyes brightened, he gasped, straightened himself, and tossed it down his throat. Then he came out, and he sighed as one who has just had a glimpse of paradise. Then he walked away with swift and resolute step, as if purposed to achieve something mighty. Only a few yards further along the road, but across the way, there stood another public house. The man walked straight to the door, entered, and took another glass, again with a quick gasp of anticipation, and again with that sigh, as of a hurried peep through the gates barred with the sword of fire. ... He went into twelve more public houses, each time with greater determination on his lips and greater eagerness in his eyes. The last glass, I suppose, opened these gates for him and suffered him to enter, for his lips suddenly lost their resolution, his eyes lost their lustre, he became limp, his arms fell heavily – he was drunk, and his face was bluer than ever.

Such blueness may well have been partly due to the presence of contaminated gin, since methanol poisoning often causes the appearance of blue-tinged or excessively pale skin.

Drinking gin to excess has even given rise to the phrase 'gin drunk' referring to crazy, mean behaviour, resulting in drinkers becoming sad and weepy.

Alcoholism was prevalent in Victorian society and was highlighted in *Oliver Twist*. When visiting a tavern, Fagin notes: 'the singers ... applying themselves, in turn, to a dozen proffered glasses of spirits and water, tendered by their most boisterous admirers; whose countenances, expressive of almost every vice ... irresistibly attracted the attention, by their very repulsiveness.'

Many drinkers drank to excess. One examples is of Sarah Stokes, an elderly woman, who was brought in front of Sir Chapman Marshall at the Mansion House, charged with having 'frequently insulted Kinnersley, the Beadle of Aldgate, and threatened to beat him'. She was noted to possess a 'strong fancy for gin, which she drank when she could get it, until it stretched her in the mud, and on Monday last she was dragged out of the puddle to the watchhouse.'

Faced with few other social options, no jobs and poor housing, many out of work people resorted to drink as a way of coping with life. In George Bernard Shaw's play *Pygmalion*, first performed in public in 1913, Eliza Doolittle tells Professor Higgins and his guests that when her aunt was dying of influenza, her father 'kept ladling gin down her throat' in a bid to help her. When Professor Higgins' guests expressed concern about this practice, indicating that it might not have been a good thing, Eliza stated that 'gin was mother's milk to her' and that as her father 'poured so much down his own throat, he knew the good of it'. She adds that her father was an avid gin drinker and that

> when he was out of work, my mother used to give him fourpence and tell him to go out and not come back until he'd drunk himself cheerful and loving-like. There's lots of women has to make their husbands drunk to make them fit to live with. You see, it's like this. If a man has a bit of a conscience, it always takes him when he's sober; and then it makes him low-spirited. A drop of booze just takes that off and makes him happy.

Drinking too much gin can cause a nasty hangover and the traditional remedy for that is to drink some more. Science has revealed why this has sometimes helped. Chemicals known as congeners are present in alcohol. Congeners have an effect on both the body and the brain, diluting the blood vessels. If a drink contains too many congeners, it can make the hangover worse. Gin is colourless and possesses far fewer congeners than any dark spirits, so has a lower effect for a short period of time, but ultimately will only delay the symptoms and may extend the hangover. This is particularly true if drinking stronger, naval-strength, gins.

The sight of females drinking spirits, often to excess, has come under particular criticism since the eighteenth century because it was regarded as being 'unwomanly'. In 1918, women working in Woolwich were secretly observed by officers making a report on 'drinking conditions among women and girls'. They were horrified to note between 4 April and 1 May 1918 the sight of women queuing for 'bottles of spirits on Fridays and Mondays', adding that 'on these days we have seen such scrambles for the limited supply of bottles, that until the women tore off the wrappers from the bottles, they did not know whether they paid 10/6 for gin, whisky or rum.'

Gin and children

In recent years, medical historians have turned to the eighteenth-century Gin Craze to seek evidence that characteristics of foetal alcohol syndrome were known long before the disease was named in 1973. Alvin Rodin pointed to Hogarth's *Gin Lane* illustration as being evidence of this. Writing in an article entitled *Infants and Gin Mania in Eighteenth Century London* published by Wright State University School of Medicine, Ohio, Rodin refers to the child falling from the drunken woman's arms as possessing 'a shorter than normal palpebral fissure [eye opening] resulting in relatively round "Orphan Annie" eyes'. He acknowledges that this is the only such example to be found in any of Hogarth's illustrations and commentators have pointed out that a more likely reason for the wide eyes could well have been much simpler – pure, stark terror, on finding himself falling head first on to the ground.

Contemporary observers such as Thomas Wilson, author of *Distilled Spirituous Liquors The Bane of the Nation* (1736), claimed that gin drinking while pregnant resulted in the birth of shrivelled children, even though they themselves had not actually seen such babies. Wilson based his remarks on a belief that prenatal exposure to 'hot spirituous liquors' could only result in 'children coming into the world half burnt up'.

Henry Fielding based his opinions on those of Wilson, rather than direct evidence, when writing his *Enquiry into the Causes of the Late increase of Robbers* in 1751 and asking 'What must become of the Infant who is conceived in Gin?' The Royal College of Physicians warned that gin drinking was 'too often the cause of weak, feeble and distemper'd children'. In 1751, the House of Commons was told that gin drinking was causing an increase in infant mortality, with estimates being made that the deaths of most premature babies was due to gin, and was also causing a decrease in the number of births. None of these statements was supported by facts or statistics.

Nowadays, other factors are also taken into account when considering the historical effects of gin drinking on babies and children. Babies from all ranks of society experienced a low survival rate. Even well-to-do families could expect that up to 75 per cent of young children might die before reaching 5 years of age. Many people lived in extremely unsanitary, overcrowded conditions and used contaminated water supplies, which led to frequent outbreaks of cholera. Starvation was common among poorer families, while diseases like measles, smallpox, tuberculosis and asthma were endemic.

Then there were the problems caused by wet nurses, who gave infants gin and water to drink, or even killed them through neglect. The practice of using wet nurses to feed young babies had become the norm among the aristocracy and affluent families, as women preferred to avoid breast feeding their children. By the mid–1700s, almost any working woman with milk in her breasts would be employed as a wet nurse. In 1711, an article in the *Spectator* referred to such women as being 'indigent'. As demand for wet nurses increased, so more and more of the poorer women became involved. Many would be drunk, or use alcohol as a pacifier. By 1753, it was noted by James Nelson, that 'there was a practice among the vulgar still more shocking ... That of giving drams to the children themselves, even while infants; they ... Pour the deadly poison down the poor babe's throat even before it can speak'. If anyone queried such deaths, the usual explanation given was that the child had suffered convulsions. His comments were echoed in 1757, when there were reports that

> A prodigious number of children are cruelly murdered by those infernals called nurses. These infernal monsters throw a spoonful of gin, spirits of wine or Hungary water down a child's throat, which instantly strangles the babe. When searchers come to inspect the body, and inquire what distemper caused the death, it is answered 'convulsions'.

It was not just wet nurses who relied on gin. Childminders were also affected. Mary Estwick, an elderly childminder, came home at two in the afternoon, 'quite intoxicated with Gin, sate down before the fire, and it is supposed, had the child in her lap, which fell out of it on the hearth, and the fire catched hold of the child's clothes and burnt it to death.' Estwick slept through the whole event in a stupor even though neighbours came in to try to rescue the baby. Estwick was reported to be 'so intoxicated, she knew nothing of what had been done'. The neglect of the child in her care was said to be directly caused by her addiction to gin.

Drunken midwives often attended women in childbirth. In *Martin Chuzzlewit*, Dickens writes about Sairey Gamp, a gin-loving midwife who drinks too much Mother's Ruin. She states, 'Mrs Harris, I says, "leave the bottle on the chimney-piece, and don't ask me to take none, but let me put my lips to it when I am so disposed, and then I'll do what I'm engaged to do.'"

Women seeking to rid themselves of unwanted babies have also turned to gin as a solution. This has been suggested as one of the reasons why Gin is sometimes described as 'Mother's Ruin'. Juniper, the key ingredient of gin, has long been known as an abortifacient. In the seventeenth century, for example, Nicholas Culpepper referred to the danger juniper posed to pregnant women because it resulted in 'speedy delivery' at any stage of a pregnancy.

As late as the 1950s, gin was being used as an abortifacient. In his 1958 novel, *Saturday Night and Sunday Morning*, novelist Alan Sillitoe refers to a factory worker, Arthur Seaton, who has an affair with his best friend's wife, Brenda. Brenda becomes pregnant. Arthur seeks help from his Aunt Ada, who recommends that Brenda should 'take a hot bath with hot gin. Tell her to stay here for two hours, as hot as she can bear it, and drink a pint of gin. That should bring it off.'

Examples still occur where gin is being used in abortions. A 2019 study by A.A. Oyeniran, *Narratives of women presenting with abortion complications in Southwestern Nigeria: A qualitative study,* included references to women being told to drink gin along with various medicines. For example, Oyeniran quoted a 19-year-old student saying 'I know is alabukun and Andrew's Liver Salts and she said I should use it with Regal dry gin, but the rest of the drugs I don't know their names.'

Gin and medicine

Juniper berries, the main constituent of gin, have played a major role in medicine and the maintenance of health for centuries. An Egyptian papyrus from 1500 BC noted that juniper berries were good for curing tapeworm infestations. In AD 64, Pedanius Dioscorides, a Roman physician, wrote about the medical uses of juniper in his book *De Materia Medica*, recommending a mixture of juniper and wine to cure a common cold.

In 1055, the monks of Salerno were known to be drinking juniper-infused wine. The medieval period saw every religious house possessing its own apothecary, while castles, large houses and even yeoman farmers had still rooms, usually supervised by the womenfolk, creating potions and medicines. Herb lore was well established throughout society and juniper was regarded as an extremely important ingredient. In 1502, herbalist John Gerard stressed the value of juniper in

> cleansing the liver and kidnies, provoking urine, a remedy against coughing and pestilential fevers, with the smoke of the leaves and wood used for driving away serpents, plague and corruption in the air, burned bark ashes in water to take away scurf of the skin, kill worms, stay the menses, and haemorrhoids, and dries ulcers.

The plague doctors

When treating plague victims, doctors commonly wore strange beak-shaped masks filled with juniper berries, as it was believed that the plague was spread by bad smells. People began eating juniper, drinking wine infused with juniper, bathing in juniper and covering themselves with juniper oil. People were often advised to burn juniper branches at least twice a day to 'protect against the epidemic'. It is debatable as to just how effective such measures were, but it is known that juniper oil acts as a natural flea repellent and rat fleas were one of the main ways in which the plague spread.

Liquorish Tooth, a Whitby-based gin company, has incorporated this image into its marketing literature and bottle labels. As Liquorish Tooth explains:

> Plague doctors were referred to as a 'Mask'd Peste' and they wore a mask that looks eerily like a bird, with herbs and spices in the beak to supposedly prevent infection. It was these herbs and spices that served as the starting point for the

ingredients for the drinks, and each bottle has the distillery's Mask'd Peste logo on it, as well as a lucky toad. During the plague, doctors would also wear a toad around their neck as they believed this would also fight off the disease, so each bottle has its own lucky toad around its neck!

Nicholas Culpepper extended the use of juniper even further in his 1652 compendium, *The English Physician*. He stated that there was, 'scarce a better remedy for win in any part of the body, or the cholic, than the chymical oil drawn from the berries'. In addition, Culpepper went on to recommend them for other ailments as they

are admirable good for a cough, shortness of breath, and consumption, pains in the belly, ruptures, cramps and convulsions. They give safe and speedy delivery to women with child, they strengthen the brain, exceedingly help the memory and fortify the sight by strengthening the optik nerves; are excellent good in all sorts of agues; they help the gout, and sciatica, and strengthen all the limbs of the body.

Distillations involving juniper were frequently created whether by apothecaries, doctors or by home distilling – a practice carried out by women. In the early seventeenth century, Sir Hugh Plat published a recipe book entitled, *Delightes for Ladies to Adorne their Persons, Tables, Closets and Distillatories*, which included a recipe featuring botanicals used in modern gin. It read:

Spirits of Spices: Distill with a gentle heat either in a balneo, or ashes, the strong and sweete water wherewith you have drawen oile of cloves, mace, nutmegs, juniper, Rosemarie, &tc after it hath stoode one moneth close stops, and so you shall purchase a most delicate spirit.

Only a few years later, in 1615, Gervase Markham wrote *The English Huswife*, a guide to household management which included numerous suggestions for aqua vitae, which women could make up to cope with ailments like wind, colic, coughs and heart infections.

Writing in his diary on 10 October 1663, Samuel Pepys noted he had been recommended to use juniper water to improve his poor constitution. He wrote that in an attempt to 'make myself break wind and go freely to stool', his friend Sir William Batten 'did advise me to take some ... strong water made of juniper'. By 1729, a report presented to Parliament referred to 'Cholick Water, which in sort was Genever' as remedy for numerous digestive problems.

While acclaimed as a medicine, gin has also been accused of causing all manner of illnesses. Achieving a balance between the two is not easy, as John Wesley acknowledged in his sermon on 'The Use of Money'. He stated:

> We may not sell anything which tends to impair health. Such is eminently all that liquid fire, commonly called drams or spirituous liquors. It is true these may have a place in medicine ... Therefore such as prepare and sell them only for this end, may keep their conscience clear ... but all who sell them in the common way, to any that will buy, are poisoners-general. They murder His Majesty's subjects by wholesale, neither does their eye pity or spare. They drive them to hell, like sheep.

The universal cure-all

Gin, rather than infusions of juniper, soon became a common remedy, a cure-all for the poorer classes in society. They would take gin to help them through the day, or to cope with ailments of all kinds. Water with gin was given as a remedy for fever, whatever the age of the patient:

adult, child or baby. In *Oliver Twist*, Charles Dickens highlights several references to the use of gin and water. He writes: 'Mr Sikes, being weak from the fever, was lying in bed, taking hot water with his gin to render it less inflammatory, and had pushed his glass towards Nancy to be replenished for the third or fourth time.'

On further occasions within *Oliver Twist*, the gin is combined with other elements. In a deathbed scene we are told: 'in addition to a moderate dose of opium prescribed by the apothecary, she [the dying woman] was labouring under the effects of a final taste of gin-and-water which had been privily administered, in the openness of their hearts, by the worthy old ladies themselves.'

Even children were not exempt. Daffy's Elixir was a common remedy combining senna (a laxative) with gin. *In Oliver Twist*, a nurse states:

> 'Why, it's what I'm obliged to keep a little of in the house, to put into the blessed infants' Daffy, when they ain't well, Mr Bumble' replied Mrs Man as she opened a corner cupboard, and took down a bottle and glass. 'It's gin. I'll not deceive you, Mr B. It's gin.'

In the early twentieth century, gin was still being given to babies. A leaflet issued by Surrey council entitled 'Hints for the Care of Infants under 1 year old' expressed concern about working-class mothers, telling them not to give 'gin or other spirits without the doctor's advice'. Since seeking medical help from doctors was not cheap, it is perhaps not surprising that many mothers turned to long-standing practices within their communities.

It was not just the poorest people who felt that gin possessed health benefits. Doctors frequently regarded it as a health drink, offering almost the equivalent to multivitamins. In 1890, the *London Medical Recorder* noted that 'our attention has been recently called to the "Original Plymouth Gin". As this *Medical Recorder* will circulate

Above: Serving gin via the cat's paw in eighteenth-century London, as a way of overcoming legislative restrictions. (*Karis Youngman*)

Right: Hogarth's *Gin Lane* was a political print supporting a government measure against the unlimited sale of gin, which later became the Gin Act. (*Mary Evans Picture Library*)

Smugglers seeking to avoid capture by pretending to rake the moon in a pool of water so as to fool the excisemen. (*Karis Youngman*)

People deliberately tried to avoid seeing smugglers moving goods by night from remote bays. That way they could truthfully say that they had seen nothing. (*Karis Youngman*)

Remote bays such as Robin Hood's Bay in North Yorkshire were ideal for landing smuggled goods, especially barrels of gin. (*Karis Youngman*)

Underground streams beneath interlinked cellars provided a way for smuggled goods to move from the bottom to the top of Baytown, at Robin Hoods Bay, without ever seeing daylight. Thus making it harder to be caught. (*Karis Youngman*)

The Gin Juggarnath, or the Worship of the Great Spirit of the age – a satire on gin's apparent grip on British life in the early nineteenth century. (*Mary Evans Picture Library*)

Tom and Jerry take Blue Ruin, or gin, in a London gin palace. (*Mary Evans Picture Library*)

Right: A plague doctor wearing a beak shaped mask filled with juniper berries to avoid infection. (*Karis Youngman*)

Below: The Mob Museum in Las Vegas charts the way the illicit liquor trade led to the growth of criminal gangs across America. (*The Mob Museum*)

Above: A display at the Mob Museum showing how all members of the community were involved in creating bootleg liquor, including children. (*The Mob Museum*)

Left: Naval hero Skip, who created legendary home-made gin that helped to boost morale among ratings and fellow officers while serving overseas. (*Hawthorn's Gin*)

Above left: Hawthorn's Gin – a grandson's tribute to a naval hero made using botanicals that would have been familiar to those that Skip sourced on his travels. (*Hawthorn's Gin*)

Above right: The first gin to be distilled on a cruise liner, the label is shaped like a gin pennant, a traditional naval symbol of hospitality. (*Salcombe Gin*)

Victorian surrealism with a hammerhead shark butler, octopus and penguins, all brought to life in a Hendricks' animated 2020 TV advertisement. (*Hendricks Gin*)

Left: The idiosyncratic Pickering's Marvellously Mixed Musical Martini Maker Mark 11. (*Pickering's Gin*)

Below: A Japanese airport fire engine re-engineered as a Pickering's Gin Thirst Extinguisher. (*Pickerin'gs Gin*)

The Tip Top Tippling Trunk – essential kit for a botanical engineer gin salesman. (*Pickering's Gin*)

Ginette the Monkey Bike – the smallest mobile gin bar in the world. (*Pickering's Gin*)

Combining the strange world of the pandemic with the iconic, dark and crazy world of Alice in Wonderland led to the creation of Gyre & Gimble's gin range. (*Karis Youngman*)

Above left: Ian Puddick and Michael Portillo beside the controversial reconstructed Miss M's Bakery wall sign at the Old Bakery Gin premises. (*Old Bakery Gin*)

Above right: TV personality and former Conservative MP Michael Portillo visiting the pop up bar at Old Bakery Gin. (*Old Bakery Gin*)

Above left: A unique Fallen Angel bottle makes this gin instantly memorable and collectable. (*Fallen Angel Gin*)

Above right: Death drinking gin at an Australian graveyard, as part of Death Gin's marketing campaign. (*Karis Youngman*)

A *Dragons' Den* near disaster turns into triumph for Liam & Mark of Didsbury Gin, when Jenny Campbell became their dragon. (*Didsbury Gin*)

THE ORIGINAL

— OCASIONALLY USED AS AN AFTERSHAVE —

BARBER'S GIN

— CUT & DISTILLED IN THE CITY —

LONDON DRY GIN

EXT. DRY

Until 1745, surgeons and barbers worked side by side. From this year onwards, King George II of Great Britain took the initiative to make a distinction between the two professions and separated the two roles accordingly, resulting in the barbers' responsibilities being limited to the cutting and styling hair and shaving.

Despite this, many barbers managed to preserve a particular method widely used in these revoked medical functions which involved the use of gin, the alcoholic drink of that particular period, as a lotion for shaving purposes.

Gin was thus incorporated into the practices of some of the most renowned barbers, bringing an air of freshness and aroma to their services.

Due to its organoleptic properties and unique manufacturing process, Barber's gin is a gin which continues to epitomise the traditional English standards of the period.

It is produced in London employing artisanal techniques and is distilled in traditional stills.

Like the gins of that era, Barber's gin does not contain citric botanicals, which in turns allows purists to serve it as recommended by us; simply gin and tonic, nothing more. However, if a touch of citrus flavour is desired, fresh lemon or orange peel can always be added to the Gin&Tonic.

— **IMPORTED** —

PRODUCT OF ENGLAND

BARBER'S GIN IS NOT AN AFTER SHAVE LOTION...
ALTHOUGH SOMEONE CAN USE IT OCCASIONALLY AS SUCH

Left: Eighteenth-century barbers sold gin as well as cutting hair. This modern Barber's Gin reflects that history. (*Barber's Gin*)

Below left: Waving a wand allows a gin based Unicorn Blood Cocktail to be served at The Cauldron, London. (*The Cauldron*)

Below right: A werewolf serves gin to visitors at The Cauldron, London (*The Cauldron*)

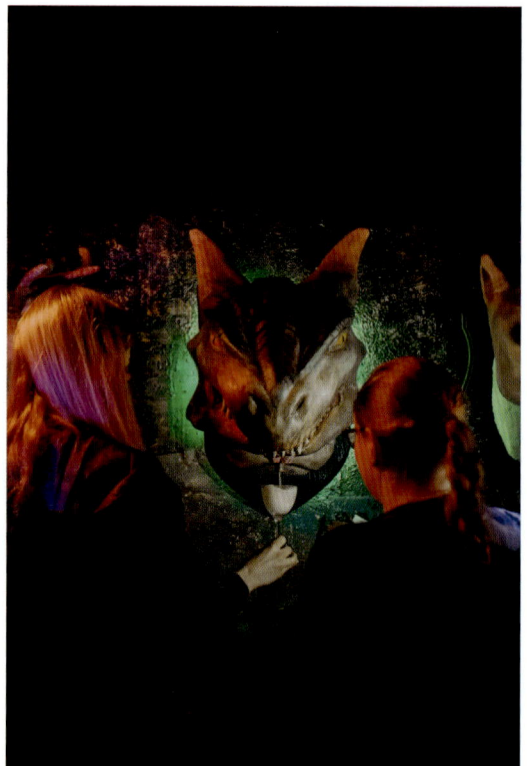

Right: A textured bottle reminiscent of the scales on a Mermaid's tail was inspired by the local legend of a mermaid's kiss. (*Mermaid Gin*)

Below left: A witch casting bespoke cursed enchantments on Evil Spirit Gin, under the light of a full moon. (*Moonpig/Brands2Life*)

Below right: Evil Spirit Gin uses apples and mint summoned from the soil of England's most haunted village. (*Moonpig/Brands2Life*)

The spirit of Nottingham, Sherwood Forest and Robin Hood is brought alive in this acorn infused gin. (*Castlegate Gin*)

Irreverent and unorthodox Bloody Merry Gin – 'two parts Jeeves & Wooster insanity, one part Art Nouveau, with a jigger of *Mad* magazine thrown in'. (*Denomination Design Australia*)

Above: Reinventing an old idea to cope with a new problem – serving gin samples via York Gin's Puss 'n' Mew machine. (*York Gin*)

Right: Silent Pool Distillers launched the world's first ever gin to come in a recyclable paper bottle. (*Silent Pool Distillers*)

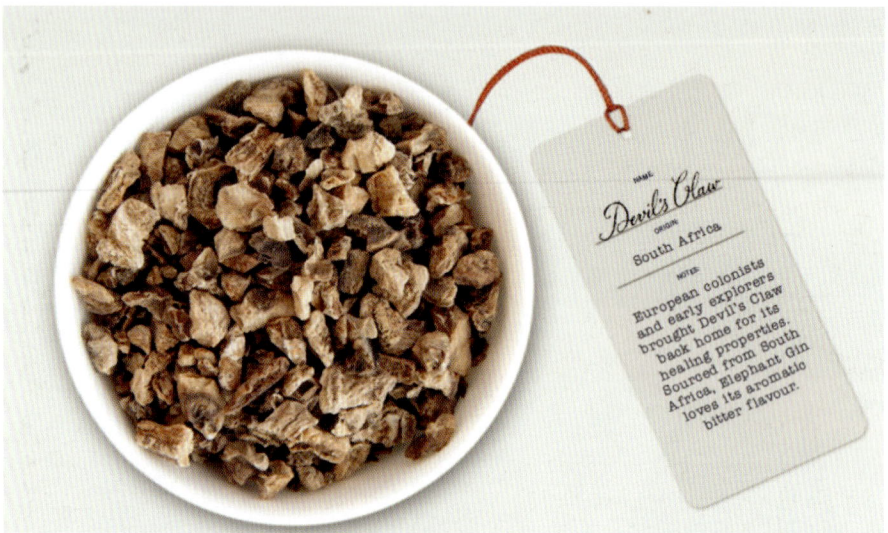

Above and below: Native African botanicals used in creating Elephant Gin link to local traditions and heritage. (*Elephant Gin*)

Elephant Gin packaging designed to attract attention to both the gin and elephant conservation. (*Karis Youngman*)

among the profession in India, we have no hesitation in calling attention to its value for medicinal, as well as general use.'

The late nineteenth and twentieth centuries witnessed a massive explosion in advertising material for the gin industry. Posters and newspaper adverts frequently portrayed gin as an ideal way of dealing with the snuffles and discomfort caused by the common cold. One such advert showed a bottle of Gordon's Dry Gin, adjacent to a kettle, sugar lumps, spoon and a glass accompanied by the words: 'A wine glass of Gordon's Dry Gin, A Slice of Lemon, A Lump of sugar, Hot Water. Take when retiring Aromatic – Refreshing – Soothing!'

In the 1930s, Gordon's Gin was promoted as being a gin with medicinal properties, perfect for dealing with depression and unhappiness. A vintage advert from the period shows two women chatting. One woman is sitting down, looking really depressed and unhappy, while her companion is standing nearby and saying, 'My dear, why don't you do as I suggest? Let me get you a drop of Gordon's out of the bottle in the sideboard. You will find it will put you right at once, and is far more pleasant to take.'

Another advertisement, for Crystal Court Gin, contained a black and white line drawing of wine glasses together with bottles of gin, plus the words: 'Pleasant Medicine Well or Ill, Pure Gin is highly beneficial'.

More controversially, gin has also been recommended as the answer to other problems like unhappiness and lack of sexual desire. In America, a late nineteenth-century poster from Minnesota, showing a woman sitting down, balancing her chair on its back legs, looking a little the worse for wear and drinking gin and tea recommended: 'Where singleness is bliss, 'Tis folly to be wives.'

Over in St Louis, Missouri, a trade card for Black Cock Vigor Gin promised drinkers countless medicinal advantages. One page read: 'Enjoy the Pleasures of Life and Keep Young by drinking Black Cock Vigor Gin' indicating it was a cure for 'Kidney, bladder and urinary troubles'.

Other sections on the trade card hint at its use in dealing with sexual problems. Accompanying the words 'For a Night Cap try Black Cock Vigor Gin' is an image of a girl dressed in transparent clothing, hiding a bottle of gin behind her back, as her lover enters the bedroom.

One of the more unexpected medicinal uses of gin was linked to cholera, a potentially deadly disease causing severe vomiting and diarrhoea, which is particularly associated with drinking contaminated water. It is estimated that there are around 2.9 million cases and 950,000 deaths each year around the world. During the nineteenth century, there were major outbreaks throughout the UK. The first outbreak took place in Sunderland in October 1831, when a ship docked in port. Many of its crew were suffering from cholera. The disease spread rapidly through the town, and eventually nationwide. The worst outbreaks were in London, where the polluted rivers caused major problems. During the 1848–9 outbreak in London, 14,137 people died. Between 1853 and 1854 another 10,738 died from a further outbreak. The disease was believed to be caused by bad smells or 'miasma' in the atmosphere, a theory supported by Florence Nightingale. Three men proved otherwise – Dr John Snow, Reverend Whitehead and Joseph Bazalgette. Snow's research into the cholera outbreak at Broad Street, Soho (during which over 600 people died in two months), was presented to the St James Parish Vestry (the organisation responsible for the health of Soho citizens) with the help of Reverend Henry Whitehead proving that it was a waterborne disease, linked to various water supplies from the wells in Soho. It was only when politicians were forced to act due to the effects of 'The Great Stink' caused by the heavily polluted River Thames, that action was taken and Joseph Bazalgette became involved to develop sewage systems that led to the triumph over 'King Cholera'. Other towns and cities quickly took similar action.

In Swansea, local man Peter Wakely theorised that since spring water and herbs were a proven remedy for cleansing and dressing wounds to prevent infection, a similar method might work inside the body. As he worked on the docks and had access to ships coming from over the world, he had no problem obtaining the necessary ingredients but needed a way to infuse them. William Lee, another local man, was renowned for distilling grain spirits and was equally concerned about the outbreaks of sickness. Noting that he had never seen a drunkard suffering from cholera, he thought there must be a connection. Joining forces, they set out to fuse their ingredients into a suitable potion. Unfortunately, their proximity to the illness meant that they caught cholera and perished. Their families remained in the area, and over the years finally recreated the partnership in the creation of the Swansea Cygnet Distillery.

However, Wakely and Lee's beliefs have since experienced some justification. In 2011, medical researchers Janet Guthrie and Darrel O Ho-Yen published a report in the *Journal of the Royal Society of Medicine* on the subject of 'Alcohol and Cholera'. Inspired by reports showing the randomness of survival and death from cholera during the 1832 outbreak in Inverness, Guthrie wondered why one person survived and another did not. She found a poster from the period urging people to avoid uncooked fruits and vegetables and to drink fermented and spirituous liquors in moderation. Wondering whether alcohol made a difference, Guthrie undertook various experiments in which the cholera virus was added to water, before adding varying concentrations of Dry London Gin. The research subsequently revealed that the survival rate of the cholera virus could be affected by gin. Guthrie and Ho-Yen noted:

We found V. cholerae did not survive in 20 per cent gin at 1 hour, 18.75 per cent gin at 6 hours and 1 per cent gin at 26 hours. The results were even more dramatic with red wine, as V. cholerae did not survive in 6.25 per cent wine at thirty minutes. Alcohol was killing some of the pathogens.

Gin has also been linked to other medicinal uses, although no evidence has been presented as to their veracity. People suffering from arthritis often claim that eating gin-soaked raisins helps. The reasoning behind this idea is that juniper in the gin possesses anti-inflammatory properties, and may provide some relief in such illnesses.

In the first decades of the twenty-first century, cannabidiol (CBD) was authorised for use in foodstuffs and beverages. Cannabidiol is an active ingredient derived from the cannabis or marijuana plant (*Cannabis sativa*), and has become a popular natural remedy for common ailments like insomnia, anxiety, muscle and joint pain. Strangeways Spirits and Muhu Spirits launched the first CBD-infused gins in 2019. In 2020, Silent Pool Distillers linked with American brand Green Stem to create a CBD gin aiming to be the highest quality on the market. It stated that Green Stem's advanced extraction methods enabled each bottle to be infused with a high level 200mg dosage of cannabidiol per bottle, compared to 10mg used by other companies. Such high quality CBD gin aims to bring a 'natural, subtle balance to the body's natural systems with every refreshing sip'. Green Stem's Simon Horth commented that the 'cloudiness of any CBD product is the best way to recognise the potency of the dosage. Many brands that claim to have CBD in their products only use minuscule amounts, rendering its effect void.'

As alcoholism remains a major problem, some companies have been inspired to create non-alcoholic versions of gin and tonic. Sea Arch Drinks uses its trademark Coastal Juniper distilled spirit as the base for an alcohol-free cocktail. Co-founder Sarah Yates says:

> Bursting with seaside botanicals, our Sea & T has all the deliciousness of a G&T with none of the alcohol. It's a great addition to the Sea Arch range as the convenient format of a 'ready to drink' can means people can simply snap it open and serve making it an easy option for occasions when you

might be driving or working. Made using traditional copper pot and steam distillation techniques, each of the ingredients is individually distilled. The process involves maceration, heating and condensing to capture the full flavour of each of the botanicals including juniper, bitter grapefruit, blood orange, coriander, cardamom, sugar, kelp and samphire to provide a genuine non-alcoholic alternative for gin lovers.

Chapter 6

Prohibition

History shows that whenever a government tries to stop or restrict people from the pleasure of drinking, drinkers will still seek to find a way to enjoy their chosen beverage. All too frequently, it also results in the involvement of criminals taking advantage of the opportunity to provide the required products. During the twentieth century, the realities of Prohibition became only too clear: it could be deadly.

Excessive consumption of alcoholic spirits has long been criticised and calls made for its abolition. During the eighteenth-century Gin Craze, John Wesley, founder of the Methodist church, stated categorically in 1743 that 'buying, selling and drinking of liquor, unless absolutely necessary, were evils to be avoided'.

The call for abolition was strongest in America where heavy drinking had long been common. Alcohol was widely available, and drinking was the norm. By 1830, it was reported that most American men aged 15 and over drank at least 7 gallons of alcohol every year.

The concept of teetotalism emerged in 1840, when six alcoholics in Baltimore, Maryland founded the Washingtonian Movement, a precursor of the modern-day Alcoholics Anonymous organisation. The Washingtonian Movement set out to teach people to be sober and become teetotal, avoiding all alcohol. It became quite powerful, impacting on all aspects of life including state governments. As early as 1845, the Maine legislature officially prohibited the sale of alcohol. Other states soon followed Maine's example, but it did not prove a long-lasting measure. Riots broke out, and in the face of widespread opposition, the legislation was soon repealed.

Despite this lack of success, the Temperance Movement and the call for total abolition continued to be a major influence on American society. Women were loudest in its support, due to the fact that the impact of excessive alcohol affected every aspect of their lives. Alcoholic husbands abused their wives, caused financial problems for women trying to feed and clothe children, made home life extremely difficult, and ultimately often led to starvation and homelessness. Encouraging temperance and abstinence from alcohol was regarded as a feminine duty. By the early years of the twentieth century, the Temperance Movement was steadily gaining strength throughout America. As a result, in 1919 the Volstead Act, formally known as the National Prohibition Act enforcing the Eighteenth Amendment, prohibiting the manufacture and sale of alcoholic beverages came into force. Andrew Volstead, a member of the House of Representatives stated: 'The American people have said that they do not want any liquor sold, and they have said emphatically by passing almost unanimously the constitutional amendment.'

Prohibition officially came into effect on 16 January 1920, and officials quickly began seizing alcohol. In New York City, barrels of beer were poured down the drains, while in Boston, pedestrians were seen walking through layers of smashed glass and liquor. Gallons of alcoholic beverages across the country were destroyed, as bars and saloons closed.

Almost immediately the Act became law, it was stridently opposed. Keen drinkers and alcohol suppliers quickly took advantage of the numerous loopholes in the legislation. Sacramental wine for religious purposes could be sold, and drug stores (pharmacies) could legally sell 'medicinal alcohol' for treating illnesses like toothache and influenza. The US Treasury Department provided doctors with official prescription forms for the provision of medicinal liquor allowing them to prescribe alcohol for their patient's health and wellbeing. Officially, a total of twenty-seven medical ailments could be treated with a drink of alcohol, including pneumonia, high blood pressure, cancer and depression. However, doctors did not have to be specific as to the treatments for which the alcohol was being prescribed. One doctor in Providence, Rhode Island simply listed the general term 'debility' on his ledger whenever he issued a prescription for alcohol. Each prescription could only be filled once at the pharmacy.

It became a popular and lucrative business. Daniel Okrent, author of *Last Call: The Rise and Fall of Prohibition*, notes that around 15,000 doctors applied for prescription permits within the first six months of Prohibition being imposed. Between 1921 and 1926, 64,000 doctors gained the right to prescribe alcohol. The amount of alcohol being prescribed in this way was considerable. In 1920 alone, doctors prescribed approximately 8 million gallons of medicinal alcohol. Nor was it just doctors who could provide such a prescription – dentists, veterinarians and pharmacists were also allowed to do so. Novelist F. Scott Fitzgerald includes references to buying alcohol at pharmacies in his book *The Great Gatsby*. Many pharmacists became extremely wealthy as a result. The Walgreen pharmacy chain expanded rapidly from 20 stores to 525 during the 1920s, although Walgreens claim this was ostensibly due to the popularity generated by the introduction of a very different type of product: milkshakes.

Prescriptions allowed patients to buy a pint of alcohol every ten days. Such prescriptions were often accompanied by instructions to 'Take three ounces every hour for stimulant until stimulated.' Not unsurprisingly, many patients were only too pleased to pay doctors $3 for a prescription, plus a further $3 or $4 at the drugstore for the alcohol. The medicinal alcohol bottles even came with a useful dosage cup fixed to the top so that drinkers could avoid drinking too much.

One of the notable celebrities who made good use of this medicinal alcohol allowance was Winston Churchill, who frequently crossed the Atlantic to give lectures in Prohibition-era America. During one such tour in 1931, he was involved in an accident in New York. He obtained a prescription from his physician, Dr Otto C. Pickhardt, which stated: 'This is to certify that the post-accident convalescence of the Hon. Winston S. Churchill necessitates the use of alcoholic spirits especially at meal times. The quantity is naturally indefinite but the minimum requirements would be 250 cubic centimetres.' The doctor added a hand written note on the prescription saying 'Keep on hand'.

Counterfeit prescriptions were common. In 1931, 400 pharmacists and 1,000 doctors found themselves caught up in a scheme involving the use of signed counterfeit prescriptions being sold to bootleggers. Surprisingly, only twelve doctors and thirteen pharmacists were ever officially charged, and were each fined just $50.

Prohibition and organised crime

Crime rates rose as a direct result of the imposition of Prohibition. Until this time, mob and gang criminals had existed on the edges of society, and had not previously been heavily involved in the manufacture, sale and distribution of alcohol. Prohibition introduced a massive change as the Las Vegas-based Mob Museum points out:

> Prohibition practically created organised crime in America. It provided members of small-time street gangs with the greatest opportunity ever – feeding the need of Americans coast to coast to drink beer, wine and hard liquor on the sly. Organised racketeers dominated the illegal 'bootlegging' industry as well as the urban machine 'bosses' and the vice kings. They understood banking and other legitimate business and bribed policemen, judges, juries, witnesses, politicians and even Federal Prohibition agents as the cost of doing business.

The resultant inter-gang rivalries became extremely violent as they fought over what they regarded as their territory for the distribution and provision of alcohol. Gang-based shootings, bombings and killings on a large scale became a common feature of 1920s' America. Over 1,000 people were killed in New York alone due to Mob activity. It led to the creation of large gangs such as the Purple Gang in Detroit, and the Mayfield gang in Cleveland. New York and Chicago saw the creation of the largest crime syndicates of all, such as the New York-based Gambino, Genovese, Lucchese, Bonnano and Colombo families.

The story of Charles 'Lucky' Luciano is typical of this Mob family growth. An Italian immigrant from Sicily, he was working for an illegal gambling boss named Arnold Rothstein when Prohibition was introduced. Rothstein quickly became involved in bootlegging, introducing Luciano to this new business opportunity. Luciano learned fast. By the mid-1920s, Luciano had proved so successful that he had become a multi-millionaire and was New York's top bootlegger making and importing alcohol. In 1931, he arranged for the death of Guiseppe 'Joe the Boss' Massaria. As a result, Luciano became the undisputed ruler of the New York Mafia.

Another example is that of Johnny Torrio and Al Capone, who ran the bootlegging, brothels and gambling gang known as Outfit, in downtown Chicago. Although they had struck a deal with other Chicago gangs to share the income from bootlegging, gang shoot-outs continued to break out over the illicit liquor trade. Between 1922 and 1926, 315 mobsters were killed during these inter-gang shoot-outs, while police officers killed a further 160. In 1929, the notorious St Valentine's Day Massacre took place. It involved associates of Al Capone and a rival gang run by George 'Bugs' Moran, which was responsible for bootlegger activity on the northern side of the city. Seven of Moran's associates were shot dead in a garage, while Moran himself had decided not to attend only a few minutes earlier. Capone was suspected of orchestrating the massacre, but was never charged. News of the massacre attracted outrage across America, and helped to erode support for Prohibition. Capone was finally caught by the authorities in 1931, when he was convicted of federal income tax evasion and had to spend eleven years in prison. During his time as a crime lord, he undoubtedly became very wealthy. Capone operated 6,000 speakeasies making more than $6m per week, while all his various businesses together were bringing in over $100m a year. Such sums far exceeded outgoings, such as paying $500,000 a month to the police to turn a blind eye to his involvement in bootlegging and illicit booze.

As the Mob Museum indicates:

> By the early 1920s, profits from the illegal production and trafficking of liquor were so enormous that gangsters learned to be more 'organised' than ever, employing lawyers, accountants, brew masters, boat captains, truckers and warehousemen, plus armed thugs known as 'torpedoes' to intimidate, injure, bomb or kill competitors. They brought in brewers closed because of Prohibition and hired experienced brewers. They sold illegal beer, watered-down whiskey and sometimes poisonous 'rotgut' booze in thousands of Mob-owned illegal bars known as speakeasies. Often to screen customers at these illegal bars, a bouncer would look through a peephole in front of the door before refusing them or letting them in.

As soon as Prohibition was imposed, many saloons were quickly transformed into speakeasies – illicit establishments selling alcohol. They became one of the worst-kept secrets of 1920s' America, existing in large numbers within every city and town. New York had more than 30,000. Also referred to as 'gin joints' and 'blind pigs', speakeasies ranged from dingy backrooms and basements to clubs complete with jazz musicians and dance floors. Some even operated as pharmacies. The Mob Museum points out that:

> Organised criminals quickly seized on the opportunity to exploit the new lucrative criminal racket of speakeasies and clubs. Organised crime in America exploded because of bootlegging. Al Capone, leader of the Chicago Outfit, made an estimated $60m supplying illegal beer and hard liquor to the thousands of speakeasies he controlled in the late 1920s.

Speakeasy owners frequently bribed police officers to look the other way, enjoy a regular drink and to give them warning whenever the Federal Prohibition agents planned a raid.

A massive quantity of alcohol was inevitably sourced illegally. Producers known as bootleggers either smuggled in liquor from elsewhere or manufactured their own. The quantities involved were immense. Some stills could make 5 gallons of liquor in eight minutes, and produced up to 100 gallons a day. In Chicago, the Genna Brothers gang employed hundreds of people to create batches of liquor in kitchens using one gallon copper 'alky cookers' (stills). The gang provided the ingredients and paid people about $15 daily to supervise the production of pure alcohol. Over in New York, gangster Frankie Yale was also known to pay $15 daily to his network of Brooklyn-based Italian-American producers. A gallon of pure alcohol cost between 50 and 75 cents to produce, and was then sold in speakeasies for $6. As the resultant taste was usually unpleasant, bar tenders often blended the drink with mixers including bitters, soda, juices and fruit, thus encouraging the concept of cocktails such as the Bees Knees. Named after a dance move of the period, the Bees Knees cocktail had honey and lemon juice added to cover up the taste of bathtub gin.

Individual bootleggers could make sizeable fortunes. George Remus was a Chicago lawyer who initially defended bootleggers in court. He quickly decided he could make more money by becoming a bootlegger himself. By 1924, he had purchased fourteen distilleries within Cincinnati, ostensibly to make medicinal alcohol for sale to pharmacies. In reality, much of the alcohol was actually sold to speakeasies and other illegal dealers. He quickly acquired a fortune of around $50m. An investigation into his activities by an undercover Prohibition agent led to his capture and trial, resulting in Remus being imprisoned for three years.

Many people created their own home brews. Mathew Rowley's *Lost Recipes of Prohibition* highlights the fascinating story of Victor Lyon, a German immigrant practising as a doctor in Harlem. His story came to light when Rowley discovered a faded book, ostensibly a collection of poetry by a German-American called George Sylvester. The contents of the book told a very different story. On opening the cover, Rowley found a bootleggers' manual, a collection of recipes and notes explaining how to make alcohol. The presence of a New York Public Library call slip within the manual enabled Rowley to identify the original owner as Victor Lyon. In view of the nature of the contents, it is likely that Lyon had been extremely busy manufacturing alcohol on a large scale due to the sheer quantities contained in each recipe. Lyon's Gin recipe required the use of 80 gallons of corn spirits, 1 pint of turpentine, 8 ounces oil of juniper, 21 pounds of salt, a half-ounce of caraway, one quarter ounce oil of sweet fennel and 8 ounces cardamine. It has been estimated that these quantities would have resulted in the creation of over 100 gallons of gin.

Across America there were countless small producers, often making alcohol for their own consumption using whatever products they had at hand. Farmers were very frequently involved in such production. Stills were hidden in forests, barns, basements and attics. All they needed was a small still that could be used to ferment a mash from corn sugar, fruit, beets or even potato peel. This created 200% proof alcohol, which was then mixed with glycerine and a touch of juniper for flavouring. By diluting the mixture with water, a 'bathtub' gin was produced – the name coming from the fact that the bottles used were usually too tall for the kitchen sink and so the bathtub had to be used.

Alcohol production and distribution became a constant battle between the Federal Prohibition agents and the bootleggers. Between 1921 and 1925, Prohibition agents seized almost 697,000 stills nationwide; while between mid-1926 and mid-1929, they seized 11,416 stills, 15,700 distilleries and 1.1m gallons of alcohol.

The quality of the alcohol produced during Prohibition was variable, and often tainted. This was particularly true with regard to the millions of gallons of frequently foul-tasting bathtub gin; drinkers ran the risk of being killed, blinded or poisoned. It has been suggested that when taken into account with the amount of bootleg alcohol, such tainted drinks could well have killed over 50,000 drinkers during the 1920s. A key reason for this situation was the fact that the bootlegger often used industrial alcohol destined for fuel or medicinal supplies. The Federal Government had a long history of requiring companies making industrial alcohol to add quinine, wood alcohol, ether, benzene, methyl alcohol, carbolic acid, chloroform, camphor, acetone, iodine, mercury salts, nicotine, formaldehyde, gasoline, cadmium, brucine (a substance closely related to strychnine), iodine and ether in order to make the industrial alcohol undrinkable. Bootleggers took such contaminated alcohol and sought ways to remove these toxic additives, but were often unsuccessful.

On Christmas Eve 1926, over thirty people died in New York as a result of drinking bootleg alcohol, and more than eighty other people became seriously ill. It was one of the worst events of this kind.

The saga began when a man stumbled into the Emergency Room of New York City's Bellevue Hospital complaining that Santa Claus was following him wielding a baseball bat. Before staff realised that he was suffering from alcohol-induced hallucinations, he died. Within hours, over sixty other people had been admitted to the hospital, all seriously ill with alcohol poisoning, and eight later died. Within two days, another twenty-three had been affected. It was clear that there was a major problem with illegal alcohol. Tests revealed traces of the poisonous materials added to the industrial alcohol on government orders. Public Health Officials and the public were horrified. At a press conference, Charles Norris, the New York City Medical examiner stated:

> The government knows that it is not stopping drinking by putting poison in alcohol. Yet it continues its poisoning process, heedless of the fact that people determined to drink are daily absorbing that poison. Knowing this to be true, the United States Government must be charged with the moral

responsibility for the deaths that poisoned liquor causes, although it cannot be held legally responsible.

His department issued public warnings, indicating that 'practically all the liquor that is sold in New York today is toxic.' It was not only the deaths over Christmas 1926 that were caused by toxic alcohol. Throughout the year, there had been a total of 1,200 people made ill and 400 deaths due to poisoned alcohol. In 1927, the number of such deaths rose to 700. Similar figures were experienced throughout the rest of the United States, and the amount of criticism increased. Anti-Prohibition legislators campaigned for a halt in the use of such chemicals. Senator James Reed of Missouri commented: 'Only one possessing the instincts of a wild beast would desire to kill or make blind the man who takes a drink of liquor, even if he purchased it from one violating the Prohibition statutes.'

Despite the growing outrage, the US Federal Government maintained its policy and sought to make it even harder for bootleggers to remove the toxic chemicals. In 1927, it ordered industrial alcohol producers to double the amount of wood alcohol content, and to add kerosene and pyridine to the chemical mix.

Smuggling alcohol was another massive source of income for the crime gangs. Boats were in operation across the oceans and lakes, buying alcohol sourced from numerous countries, especially the UK and Canada. In Cleveland, Moe Dalitz's Mayfield Road Gang operated speed boats bringing in Canadian alcohol across Lake Erie. Some boats smuggled alcohol ashore ready for distribution in the classic smuggling style, while other boats simply moored up in international waters. These moored boats led to the creation of the term 'rum running' as it involved the use of a stretch of ocean known as Rum Row, which was located 12 miles away from the US Coast in international waters. The boats possessed false bottoms creating areas in which bottles of alcohol were stored. Fish bins would be placed on top. Small high-speed boats would zoom up to the boat, throw a bundle of high denomination money on board and receive a liquor order in exchange. By 1930, the US Federal Government estimated that the smuggling of foreign made liquor into America had become a $3 billon industry.

Many states refused to enforce Prohibition or to provide money for policing the alcohol ban. Maryland was one such state, refusing to enact an enforcement code. It gained a reputation for being the most implacable anti-Prohibition state in America. The Maryland Senator William Cabell Bruce told Congress that 'National Prohibition went into legal effect upward of six years ago, but it can be truly said that, except to a highly qualified extent, it has never gone into practical effect at all.'

By the late 1920s, many American states had decreased their Prohibition activity. With the Great Depression taking hold, the USA needed the money generated by tax revenues on alcohol.

Moving such large quantities of illicit liquor around the country was not easy. America is a vast continent, therefore the liquor often had to be transported long distances, on rough roads and without lights Bootleggers moving illicit alcohol supplies around the country needed fast cars in order to avoid the police and Federal Prohibition agents. These 'souped-up' cars incorporated modified engines and improved suspension to handle the weight and speed required, while much of the interior was stripped back to provide alcohol storage space.

Edmund Fahey, of Spokane, Washington was a runner who smuggled alcohol from Canada into the USA. He later wrote that the cars were put through mechanical tests as tough as any needed by official race drivers. 'Tyres were put to the severest possible tests. Heavy loads, hauled over the toughest of roads often at reckless speeds, keep the rubber on your car always under the utmost strain ... Several companies developed tyres especially for the rum running trade. Many a runner served time in jail simply because his rubber failed him at some critical moment.'

Racing the transformed cars on makeshift tracks became a popular sporting pastime for 'runners', especially in North Carolina, Virginia, Tennessee, Georgia and other Southern States. It was a way of practising their skills and honing their driving techniques.

Officially, Prohibition lasted for just over ten years. It was officially repealed by President Roosevelt in 1932 and New York was quick to repeal its enforcement code. By 1933 the majority of American states had complied. Production of illegal liquor continued, but not in the massive quantities that had previously been the norm.

With the end of Prohibition, distilleries were quick to take advantage of the massive market for gin that had emerged during the 1920s' jazz age. Gin brands were widely advertised and extensively promoted, especially in the form of gin and tonic, or gin-based cocktails. Many of the cocktails on offer had very suggestive names such as the Tommy Rotter and the Hanky Panky. This latter drink was created by Ada Coleman for a favourite client who wanted a drink 'with a bit of a punch in it'. The rich brown tinge hinted at the possession of medicinal qualities, thus enhancing the idea that the drink was good for you.

Overall, the imposition of Prohibition was never fully successful. State governors resented the financial impact it made on state finances, due to the fact it led to the closure of many legitimate businesses. State revenues decreased dramatically since they were unable to impose taxes on alcohol production and this could involve massive sums. To take but one example, Detroit's alcohol trade pre-Prohibition had been second only to cars in terms of its economic activity.

Although the role of Prohibition within the USA is by far the most well known, other countries, such as Iceland, have made attempts to stop the sale of alcohol. A referendum in 1908 resulted in Icelanders voting in favour of a total ban on alcohol. Prohibition in Iceland was introduced in 1915, and lasted officially until March 1989, albeit with some exemptions. The ban had involved all types of alcohol until 1921, when Spain refused to buy Icelandic fish unless Iceland purchased Spanish wine. This resulted in an exemption being granted on wine sales. Spirits continued to be outlawed, except for medicinal purposes, for which alcohol could be imported. Consequently, doctors prescribed liquor, especially gin, for all types of ailments from chest pains to neurotic disorders. In 1935, a further referendum was held relating to the legislation of spirits such as gin. The Icelandic Temperance Movement managed to ensure that beer remained forbidden, arguing that beer consumption would lead to greater problems since it was cheaper to buy than spirits. In reality, the drinking of spirits increased rapidly after 1935, and it was said that many people simply aimed for oblivion when out for a drink.

The impact of the US Prohibition policies

The concept of Prohibition remains dominated by images of the American experience, possibly because it involved such dramatic and very visible effects. Quite apart from the countless references and portrayals in literature and on film, Prohibition helped to generate a very distinct form of crime novel involving mobsters and private detectives. There is little doubt that without Prohibition, the concept of the Mob and the Mafia may not have achieved the same impact or become so well known. The Prohibition era led to an explosion in the growth of organised crime, creating frameworks and cash for major crime families. Although these are far less powerful nowadays, such families and networks remain active in twenty-first-century USA.

Memories of Prohibition and its surrounding cultural aspects continue to impact on the gin industry. Tom's Town distillery is named after the USA's most corrupt political boss, Tom Prendergast, who began trading as a saloon keeper before founding a wholesale liquor company. Kansas City came under his control, and totally ignored the strictures of Prohibition, becoming known as the Paris of the Plains, where money, jazz and spirits dominated. When asked to justify his opposition to Prohibition, Prendergast said simply 'The People are thirsty.' The links between Tom's Town distillery and the Prohibition era are stressed still further by the creation of McElroy's Corruption Gin, named after the city manager, Henry McElroy. During his time in office, McElroy was involved in numerous shady contracts as well as the vice industry, alongside Tom Prendergast. The company commented that 'In McElroy's spirit we present an elaborate and cunning gin, a corruption of unexpected flavours and uncommon botanicals.'

But what of the main reason given for the imposition of Prohibition – problems caused by inebriation and alcoholism? Although well intended, the Prohibition period actually had the opposite effect. As writer Paul Mejia comments in *Gastro Obscura*:

> Alcohol enthusiasts drank more hard liquor during Prohibition than before, and spirits accounted for a staggering 75 per cent of all alcoholic beverages consumed in the United States … The era unwittingly became the foundation of contemporary American drinking culture, giving birth to libations including mixed drinks, bathtub gin and moonshine. Some might say that's just what the doctor ordered.

Chapter 7

Gin as a Fashionable Drink

With the dawn of the 1920s, gin took on a new guise. Cocktails such as gin and tonic became the drink of fashionable socialites, especially the group known as the Bright Young Things – bohemian socialites and younger aristocrats who were bent on enjoying life in the wake of the mass slaughter experienced in the First World War. Free from the restrictions that had governed the social round during Victorian times, women were relishing their new freedoms. This was the era of 'flappers', young women wearing knee-length skirts, bobbed hair, drinking cocktails and listening to jazz. Heavy drinking and drug use were common.

Criticising this new breed of gin drinkers, Sir Arthur Conan Doyle described them as 'the loungers of the Empire'. Gin was glamorous, fuelling the social life of a generation. Debutantes and Bright Young Things frequently drank Gin and It (a mix of gin and sweet vermouth) as highlighted in Evelyn Waugh's classic period tale *Brideshead Revisited*.

Jazz clubs and cocktail bars in smart hotels catering for a wealthy clientele became the hub of the social life of these Bright Young Things, who drank countless cocktails in the course of an evening. Many of the cocktails were heavy on the gin. Playwright Noel Coward defined the perfect Martini as being 'made by filling a glass with gin, then waving it in the general direction of Italy'. His play, *Words and Music* features a group of debutantes singing about gin:

The Gin is lasting out,
No matter whose,
We're merely casting out

The Blues,
For Gin, in cruel
Sober truth
Supplies the Fuel
For Flaming Youth,
A drink is known
To help a dream along
We can't refuse,
The Gin is lasting out,
We're merely casting out
The Blues!

This was a trend experienced throughout the western world. American author F. Scott Fitzgerald included numerous references to Gin Rickeys in *The Great Gatsby*. Close friends renamed Gin Rickeys as a Gin Fitzy because Fitzgerald drank so many of them. It was said that he liked gin because the smell didn't linger on the breath, no matter how much he drank. As a heavy gin drinker, he commented: 'First you take a drink, then the drink takes a drink, then the drink takes you.' Social activist and writer Dorothy Parker worked on magazines like *New Yorker*, *Vogue* and *Vanity Fair* and wrote 'I like to have a Martini, two at the very most; three, I'm under the table, four I'm under my host'. So well known was her connection with gin that her name now appears on all kinds of US gin-themed merchandise, while the New York Distilling Company has named its flagship gin Dorothy Parker.

Gin at Happy Valley, Kenya

Possibly the most notorious group of gin drinkers was to be found in Kenya. Their story had begun much earlier, in 1901, when a British aristocrat named Hugh Cholmondeley, the third Baron Delamere, moved to Kenya and acquired thousands of acres of land in the area around Lake Naivasha, the Wanjohi Valley and Aberdare mountain range. Other British and Anglo-Irish aristocrats and socialites soon followed. By the 1920s, the area had become known as Happy Valley and was a hedonistic paradise.

Inhabited by a social set relentless in the pursuit of amusement, Happy Valley was a focus for drink, drugs and sex. Hugh Cholmondeley became one of the leaders of that social set and has been credited with creating the term 'white hunter' for his exploits. There are stories of him riding his horse into the dining room of Nairobi's Norfolk Hotel and jumping over the tables, as well as knocking golf balls on to the roof of the Muthaiga Country Club before climbing up to retrieve them. Society women in Happy Valley drank their way through countless cocktails such as White Ladies and Pink Gin. Gin with orange bitters was the favourite drink of Lady Idina Sackville, while Lady June Carberry drank so much gin it was said if you 'cut her in half, you'd find mostly gin'.

Happy Valley quickly became renowned for its scandalous social behaviour. By far the biggest scandal centred around the activities of a Scottish Peer known as Josslyn Victor Hay, Earl of Errol. A renowned philanderer, he eloped with Idina Sackville (at the time married to Charles Gordon), before marrying her and settling in Kenya in 1924. Over the next few years, Josslyn and Idina became the unofficial king and queen of Happy Valley. Their home, Slains, was the centre of Happy Valley social life and notorious for wild parties, orgies, drug use and spouse-swapping sessions. Josslyn had an affair with Countess Alice de Janzé, who was described as doing 'one mile to the gallon on gin'. In 1929, Idina divorced Josslyn as he was cheating her financially.

Within a short time, Josslyn had eloped with yet another married woman, Molly Ramsey-Hill. Molly's husband was incensed and publically horsewhipped Josslyn at the Nairobi Railway Station, before divorcing his wife. As part of the resultant divorce settlement, Molly gained an elaborate property known as the Dijin Palace where she set up home with her new husband Josslyn. It became the party palace for Happy Valley. Some reports suggest that the Dijin Palace gained its name from Erroll's habit of drinking large gins. Gin and tonic was the favourite drink served, along with Pink Gins mixed with champagne for breakfast. Another characteristic feature of the palace was the fact that bedrooms could only be locked from the inside.

Following Molly's death, caused by the effects of cocktails of alcohol, morphine and heroin, Josslyn found a new lover in the form of Diana, Lady Delves Broughton. Their romance was carried out in public, and they planned to elope. It was rumoured that Diana's husband had agreed to their relationship. Then in January 1941, Josslyn was found murdered in a parked car in Nairobi. Delves Broughton was charged and tried, before being eventually acquitted due to lack of evidence. As the tales of the gin-soaked parties and erotic games enjoyed by the Happy Valley set were recounted during the trial, the resultant media coverage transfixed the attention of readers worldwide. It continues to do so, as the stories have led to numerous murder mysteries and films such as *White Mischief*, dealing with the Delves Broughton trial, and more recently the 1999 UK TV series *Heat of the Sun*.

The Second World War

Gin and tonic remained a popular drink throughout the Second World War. Noel Coward wrote: 'When the warning sounds I gather up some pillows, a pack of cards and a bottle of gin, tuck myself beneath the stairs and do very nicely … until the "all clear" sounds.' Another prominent dry Martini drinker was Winston Churchill. He and his Cabinet were often to be seen at the Dorchester, which provided access to a constant supply of Martinis. There are unconfirmed reports that when Churchill was asked how much vermouth he wanted in his Martini he commented: 'I would like to observe the vermouth from across the room while I drink my Martini.' He is also reported to have said that the only way to make a Martini was with ice-cold gin, and a bow in the direction of France.

Army officers on active service often found themselves having to create their own versions of gin. One such officer was Major Dennis Thatcher, future husband of Margaret (née Roberts). Lacking a supply of gin while serving in France, he and his colleagues made their own by mixing oil pressed from juniper berries into alcohol. Thatcher commented: 'a mouthful of this stuff nearly blew our heads off,' and that it was 'terrible stuff and tasted like hell' but they drank it anyway. With no tonic available, they added fruit juice, thus creating 'gin and jungle juice'.

Wartime films often depicted people drinking gin. In *Casablanca*, one of the most iconic of all wartime films, gin plays a major role. The classic line spoken by Rick (played by Humphrey Bogart) reflecting the arrival of his ex-lover and her new Nazi boyfriend into his bar, is well known: 'Of all the Gin joints, in all the towns, in all the world, she walks into mine.' Rick then orders a French 75 cocktail containing gin, champagne, lemon juice and sugar syrup. This is a drink said to possess a kick, like being hit by a weapon (or the shock of an ex-girlfriend appearing with a new man in her life). The name French 75 is rumoured to have been coined by Harry MacElhone (owner of Harry's American Bar in Paris) after the 75mm Howitzer gun used by the French and American armies following the First World War.

In 1949, one of the most iconic post-war books, George Orwell's *1984*, was published. Telling the story of a dystopian future, it involves an all-seeing leader known as Big Brother (which has since become a symbol for intrusive government and bureaucracy). The protagonist, Winston Smith, dreams of rebellion, remembering what life was like before the party gained power. He drinks Victory Gin, even though it is not a pleasant experience, instead just a way of surviving, gulping it down 'like a dose of medicine'. Victory Gin was the staple diet of all the workers in the Ministry of Truth.

Describing Victory Gin, George Orwell wrote that it 'was like nitric acid … In swallowing it one had the sensation of being hit on the back of the head with a rubber club. The next moment, however, the burning in his belly died down and the world began to look more cheerful'.

He continued:

> Winston sat in his usual corner, gazing into an empty glass … Unbidden, a waiter came and filled his glass up with Victory Gin, shaking into it a few drops from another bottle with a quill through the cork. It was saccharine flavoured with cloves, the speciality of the café.

> He picked up his glass and drained at a gulp. As always the gin made him shudder and even retch slightly. The stuff was horrible. The cloves and saccharin, themselves disgusting enough in their sickly way, could not disguise the flat oily smell and what was worst of all was that the smell of gin, which dwelt with him night and day, was inextricably mixed up in his mind with the smell of those … he never named them, even in his thoughts.

Gin cocktails continued to feature in many classic novels. In Raymond Chandler's *The Long Goodbye*, Terry Lennox tells detective Philip Marlowe that 'A real Gimlet is half Gin and half Rose's lime juice and nothing else. It beats Martinis hollow.'

Ernest Hemingway makes many references to gin throughout his novels, reflecting his own love of the drink. There are Harry's Bar scenes involving Martinis within his novel *Across the River into the Trees*, while in *A Farewell to Arms* his character Frederic Henry sips Martinis and says, 'I had never tasted anything so cool and clean. They made me feel civilised.' For Hemingway, drinking gin was also a way of dulling pain. Despite this, he often sought out sophisticated bars wherever he travelled, drinking cocktails such as a White Lady (gin, Cointreau and lemon juice), or more famously indulging in Martini benders with actor Spencer Tracey during the filming of *The Old Man and The Sea*.

Many post-war films include references to gin and gin-based cocktails. In Truman Capote's film, *Breakfast at Tiffany's*, Holly Golightly drinks White Angels, a mix of 'one half vodka, one half gin, no vermouth'. By far the most well-known appearance of gin cocktails, and the most frequently quoted, is in the James Bond films. Author Ian Fleming is believed to have enjoyed Martinis mixed with vodka, gin and vermouth so much that he featured it in both the novel and film of *Casino Royale*. In the original book, published in 1953, James Bond orders a Vesper Martini saying 'Three measures of Gordon's, one of vodka, half a measure of Kina Lillet. Shake it very well until it's ice cold, then add a large thin slice of lemon peel. Got it?' When it came to the films, Bond's request was much shorter, and intensely memorable. He invariably orders a dry Martini which has to be 'shaken, not stirred'.

Occultist Aleister Crowley preferred a very different form of cocktail. Addicted to heroin, he was said to go to a particular pub in Bloomsbury and order a Kublai Khan No 2 – a mix of gin and laudanum (a form of opium dissolved in sherry). The resultant concoction has been described as being the equivalent of a heroin Martini.

Despite such prominence in film and literature, gin's popularity steadily declined. It was a drink that came to represent all that was seen as wrong with austerity, wartime and social life. Gin was no longer exciting or appealing to the young people of post-war Britain. Instead, gin was regarded as old-fashioned, something drunk by parents and grandparents. It was the bottle brought out when visitors came to middle-class homes. As the years progressed, gin became increasingly associated with nostalgia, wartime, and colonialism – the somewhat reactionary Colonel Blimp mentality of people drinking gin and tonic in club houses. Hints of this transformation had begun to appear during the war years, in John Betjeman's view of Middle England. His 1941 poem, *A Subaltern's Love Song*, includes the words:

> Her father's euonymus shines as we walk,
> And sing past the summer-house, buried in talk,
> And cool the verandah that welcomes us in
> To the six-o'clock news and a lime-juice and gin.

By 1954, Noel Coward was also reflecting on its change of status, and how gin had become the drink of middle-aged women. He wrote:

> To that bar on the Piccola Marina
> Where love came to Mrs Wentworth-Brewster
> Hot flushes of delight suffused her
> Right round the bend she went, picture her astonishment
> Day in, day out she would gad about
> Because she felt she was no longer on the shelf
> Night out, night in, knocking back the gin.

Gin consumption steadily declined. Many London distilleries closed or failed to reopen after being bombed during the Second World War, leaving Beefeater and Gordon's reigning supreme. Women still tended to order it, as there was relatively little choice in drinks available – stout and gin tended to be their main choice, although by the 1960s vodka had begun to replace gin as a more fashionable drink among younger people. Among members of high society, gin continued to be popular, especially with royalty. Queen Elizabeth was known to enjoy a gin and tonic, while Queen Elizabeth the Queen Mother had a definite fondness for gin, with countless stories circulating relating to her consumption of the spirit. How many of these stories were true is hard to know, although typical stories include references to her instructing her dressers to hide bottles of gin in hatboxes when she travelled, so she could enjoy a quick drink whenever she wanted. One of her pages later auctioned a handwritten note from her relating to a picnic, which stated 'I think that I will take two small bottles of Dubonnet and gin with me this morning in case it is needed. It is a beautiful day, could we have lunch under the tree – one could have fourteen at the table and four at a small table.'

Another story of aristocrats and their gin relates that in 1961, Winston Churchill's daughter Sarah was evicted from her apartment in Dolphin Square due to her habit of hurling gin bottles out of the window.

Gin was favoured by the Cambridge spy ring headed by Soviet double agent Sir Anthony Blunt, Surveyor of the Queen's paintings. Anecdotal reports at the time refer to him leaving his apartment in the Courtauld Institute of Art every Saturday morning 'soon after opening time, shortly to struggle back with carrier-bags stuffed to bursting with gin'.

For many people, gin became a solace. Evelyn Waugh wrote:

My life is roughly speaking over ... I try to read the paper. I have some gin. I try to read the paper again. I have some more gin. I try to think about my autobiography, then I have some more gin and it's lunchtime. That's my life. It's ghastly.

Poet Philip Larkin described his perfect gin and tonic in his 1974 poem, *Sympathy in White Major*:

When I drop four cubes of ice
Chimingly into a glass, and add
Three goes of Gin, and a lemon slice,
And let a ten-ounce tonic void
In foaming gulps until it smothers
Everything else up to the edge
I lift the lot in private pledge.

Another well-known gin drinker at this time was Dennis Thatcher, the husband of Margaret Thatcher, prime minister between 1979 and 1990. An elderly reactionary, he relished a world of golf clubs and drinking gin and tonic, frequently being lampooned for this lifestyle in media such as *Private Eye* and on *Spitting Image*. Typical Dennis Thatcher comments from this period included 'I don't know what reception I'm at, but for God's sake, give me a gin and tonic,' while on a morning flight to Scotland, he told his wife 'it is never too early for a gin and tonic'. Downing Street staff recall his demand that just the cork in a bottle of Italian vermouth should be passed over his neat gin.

Above all, gin was associated with bored suburban housewives. Writing in *Gin Glorious Gin*, Olivia Williams noted how gin was 'the calling card of the unhappy middle-class women' in plays such as Alan Ayckbourn's *Absurd Person Singular*, in which one of the characters, Marion, is constantly heard grumbling that she had never had such small gins in her life as the gin was drowned by tonic. Writing in the *Spectator*, Jeffrey Barnard refers to the world of suburban housewives as being 'When the shopping's been done in Hungerford, after the obligatory weekly treat of a hair-do in Wantage, and the Mini's been safely put away in the garage, it's back to the log fire, out with the gin and away with the past.'

Gin had become the drink of boredom, and social snobbery chosen by people who wanted to appear upmarket, inhabiting a world of golf clubs and dinner parties. Olivia Williams comments:

> In the subtlety of British snobbery, it was recognised by now as a drink for people who were trying too hard to seem upmarket, rather than those who naturally were. The phrase the 'gin and Jaguar belt' came to represent the provincial nouveau riche whose heartland was the mock-Tudor architecture and manicured lawns of the Home Counties. In popular culture, they were epitomised by Margo and Jerry Leadbetter in the sitcom *The Good Life*, set in Surbiton, on the outskirts of

London. Their poorer neighbours, the Goods, remark that the only thing the Leadbetters 'buy in bulk is gin'.

In 1972, artists Gilbert and George set out to make fun of the idea of 'Englishness' by creating a video installation known as Gordon's Makes Us Drunk. It featured the elegantly dressed duo looking out over London, listening to Elgar's *Land of Hope and Glory* while slowly pouring glasses of gin. As they pour the drinks, they continually repeat the words 'Gordon's makes us drunk' and 'Gordon's makes us very, very drunk.'

Chapter 8

Naval Gin

Ships sailing across the world's oceans carried with them not just trading goods and naval power, but also gin. It was a much-desired drink; safe to consume, even when there were problems with water supplies. Organisations like the Dutch East India Company took with them their love of genever, while the Royal Navy insisted on supplies of gin. Both were much sought after at destinations en route, as well as in the ports where the vessels were based.

Many distilleries were based in maritime cities. As well as buyers, these locations provided good access for all the key ingredients needed to distil gin: grain, spices and clean flowing water. The quality of the gin was variable, and was frequently watered down by the distillers. Gin for the domestic market generally measured 44.6% proof prior to 1819, and 47.4% proof afterwards. Gin destined for the Royal Navy tended to be stronger. Having the correct strength of gin was very important. Not only did it keep the sailors happy, it was also a safety measure. Distillers creating gin for the Royal Navy were required to provide spirits that were at least 57.5% proof. This was because the gin barrels were stored below deck adjacent to the gunpowder supplies. Consequently, if the gin barrels split during the voyage, they would not contaminate the gunpowder, although it is said that even if soaked in the spirit, the gunpowder would still ignite.

As a result, it became the normal practice to test the spirits to identify their strength. This was the task of the Royal Navy Supply Officers known as the pursers (or 'pussers'). The system they used was quite simple. A mixture of gunpowder and spirits was placed in a special container and lit. If it burned with a clear flame, then it was 'proof' that the alcohol was of a sufficiently high standard. If it failed to burn, or burned with a smoky flame, it was rejected as being 'under proof'. Alternatively, if it burned with lots of smoke and exploded with a bang, then it was 'over proof' and also rejected.

There are references to gin in numerous seventeenth-century naval documents. Requests were made for supplies of 'Hollands' (Dutch gin) to be sent to the Cape of Good Hope. Another naval reference in 1799 relates to the demand for 'coarse and water', a slang term for Plymouth Gin. Many naval ships leaving Plymouth harbour took on board around 200 cases of gin for use during the voyage by the sailors on board – and it was not unknown for crews to drink every last drop before the ship had even reached Gibraltar. By the mid-eighteenth century, the Plymouth distillery was supplying 1,000 barrels of navy-strength gin to the Royal Navy every year – and this was just one of the many suppliers, albeit the most popular. During the Napoleonic Wars, Vice Admiral Horatio Lord Nelson placed an order for Plymouth Gin for consumption by his officers.

In 1864, the Dutch navy ordered that all ships should issue daily gin rations. The orders stated: 'for European, African and Ambonese non-commissioned officers and troops, and for European women; the morning 0.075 Dutch kan [about 105ml/3.7oz] of Jenever; in the afternoon 0.075 Dutch kan of Jenever; in the evening 0.075 Dutch kan of Jenever.' This amounted to approximately one-fifth of a bottle of gin per person, per day. Sailors would line up and be given a mug filled with genever by an officer. It was swallowed in one gulp, then the mug refilled and passed to the next person.

Gin and the Second World War

Events during the Second World War reflected just how important gin had become to the Royal Navy. During the Blitz, the presence of the naval dockyards in Plymouth led to the city being heavily bombed. Anecdotal reports indicated that when the fleet was notified that Plymouth, including the Plymouth Distillery, had been bombed, one sailor commented: 'Well, Hitler just lost the war.' Many years later, the granddaughter of another Second World War Royal Navy sailor visited Plymouth Distillery and retold a story about how her grandfather had written a letter commenting that bombing Plymouth was Hitler's death knell, because sailors were so incensed at the thought of the distillery being destroyed. So strong was the concern that the Royal Navy made an announcement to all ships saying that the distillery had survived the bombing and was still producing gin.

Royal Navy officers sought out bottles of gin wherever they could while serving overseas, including black market versions. This meant that the gin was not always high quality. On one occasion, future Rear Admiral Edmund Poland was serving on board HMS *Petand* when some duty free gin, purchased in Egypt, was sold on to some other ships in the fleet. He recalled, 'There was a terrible row because we were accused of having put paraffin in the gin. Of course, it wasn't us. It was the extraordinary occasion when Plymouth Gin had been contaminated and we happened to have a tremendous amount of Plymouth Gin. There was some problem with the juniper juice from North America.'

Another naval officer's wartime exploits led, many years later, to the creation of a very special gin by his grandson. Nicknamed Skip, Royal Navy Commander Michael Wallrock used to distil his own gin and take it on board. Hawthorn's Gin founder Will Turnage says:

I always knew my grandfather was a war hero, serving mostly in the Mediterranean. In 1941, he took part in the perilous Tiger Convoy and was awarded the Croix de Guerre by the French for his role in the D–Day landings in June 1944. We were very proud of him but knew little else of his life at sea. Like so many of his generation, Skip didn't talk about the war. So, when I discovered his old war diary, it was a revelation. He wrote about air raids and torpedoes; of being sunk three times and never getting his feet wet; his homesick men and playing 'ruggers' on deck; the time the King and Queen inspected the docks ... and he wrote about gin.

Skip distilled the gin himself – collecting botanicals from the far reaches of the world in which he laid anchor. He combined them with English wheat in a copper pot still to distil his legendary gin. And then he smuggled the gin on board, sharing it with 'ratings' to boost the morale of his war-ravaged crew.

Will believes that his grandfather began producing home-made gin around June 1942, and from then on it became a regular occurrence until the end of the war. As he was an officer in charge of a ship, he simply took on board all the gin that he could carry.

Will continues:

It appears as though he collected what he could, and where he could and one would assume that each batch varied from one to another. Some of his fellow officers and ratings were given gin in the Commander's quarters on top of their rum rations ... one would assume there were no complaints from anyone being given extra booze. Recreating his recipe seemed like the perfect tribute to my grandfather.

The result was The Skip. Although the exact recipe used by Skip in wartime is unknown, Hawthorn Gin created a version using botanicals that would have been familiar to Skip resulting in a well-balanced gin which could be drunk neat or with tonic.

Naval traditions

It was customary for sailors to receive a tot of gin or rum at six bells (3 p.m.) during the afternoon watch. The Up Spirits Ceremony involved the crew lining up around a barrel bearing the words, 'The King (or Queen) God bless him/her' before being served with their drink.

This 300-year-old tradition, was finally abolished on 31 July 1970 (also known as Black Tot Day) on the orders of Admiral Sir Michael Le Fanu, First Sea Lord. The decision had been made due to increasing concerns relating to drunkenness. Between 1965 and 1966, three sailors died from acute alcohol poisoning. There were forty-five serious incidents of drunkenness, and four incidents resulting in accidental death. The *Observer* wrote an opinion piece commenting on the number of Pink Gins being drunk in the Officers' Wardroom, saying, 'If their Lordships and the Admiralty thought alcohol and computer gunnery didn't mix, they should put the officers and petty officers on the wagon first.'

In true naval tradition, Black Tot Day was marked with numerous special ceremonies held on board the ships. Many of the sailors wore improvised costumes and barrels were drained, before being buried at sea. Some sailors wore black armbands, and at HMS *Collingwood*, a naval training base, there was a mock funeral procession complete with a black coffin and accompanying drummers and piper.

Another naval tradition was for newly commissioned ships to receive a gin commissioning kit. This comprised a wooden box containing two bottles of navy-strength gin and glassware. Such a kit had also been given ceremoniously to the victors in a wartime action – sink a ship or down a plane and you get some Plymouth Gin.

Although the naval tot has been abolished, spirits are still available on Royal Navy ships, although no longer a perk of the job; such drinks have to be purchased in the Mess. The only exception to this rule is when the navy orders 'splice the mainbrace', allowing every serving sailor a free ration of spirits. This order is only ever given on very special occasions, for example, the birth of Prince William in 1982; the Queen's Golden Jubilee in 2002; the Fleet Review in 2005; and the Queen's Diamond Jubilee in 2012. Only members of the Royal

Family – normally the Queen – and the admiralty board are allowed to issue that specific command.

When naval ships are cruising in a flotilla, officers keep a careful check on the flags being flown on board the other ships, in case the gin pennant is raised. If this pennant is displayed it means other ships could send their officers over for free drinks. There have been reports that it was not unknown for junior officers to try to raise a gin pennant on another ship, thus forcing that ship to issue free drinks. However, if the officers were caught raising the pennant, then it was their ship which had to bear the cost of the drinks. The tradition is still followed by some Commonwealth navies.

No one knows when this practice first began, but what made the flag extra special was the fact it was designed to be as inconspicuous as possible, thus making it harder to spot. The possibility of seeing the pennant undoubtedly helped make officers on watch much more attentive! Early gin pennants comprised a small triangular flag adorned with a white wine glass. Later designs involved a wine or cocktail glass, and became a starboard pennant.

Gin and naval imagery

Reminders of these naval links persist throughout the gin industry. Strong gins are described as naval strength. However, this has nothing to do with the navy; it is actually a marketing term coined in the 1990s to sell high-strength spirits. Naval-strength gin has to be bottled at 57.1% proof.

In the US, the Walter Collective Navy Gin bears a label stating that it is battleship grade and 'should be poured with honour, mixed with valour'. The hero on the label is a Second World War sailor named Walter, who served at various bases in America. The label is printed on both sides with information relating to his life and times, with designs capturing the wartime world of the 1940s.

Brand names are often associated with naval imagery such as Flintlock, Black Powder, Seadog and Nelson's navy-strength gin. Hayman distilleries Royal Dock Gin was named after the Royal Dock in Deptford, London which supplied the Royal Navy from 1863, while in Liverpool, Ginsmiths created a Merchant Navy Gin. Southampton-based HMS Spirits is creating a fleet of gins: Mary Rose named after the Tudor vessel, and Dreadnought reflecting the strength of the early twentieth-century naval ships. According to the founder, Ben McGuire, the creation of a HMS Fleet Gin matched his naval family background, 'encompassing integrity and respect for others, together with a real sense of adventure, and a willingness to go out there and take risks'.

Naval brand names with charitable links are common. A typical example is that of Conker Spirits, which created an RNLI Navy Strength Gin to help raise funds for the Royal Naval Lifeboat Institution. The Isle of Wight Distillery has partnered with the National Museum of the Royal Navy to produce HMS Victory Gin, 'crafted in the spirit of high seas, courage and adventure'. A proportion of the resulting profits from sales are donated to the National Museum of the Royal Navy to fund the ongoing restoration of HMS *Victory*.

Medicinal links

Naval links with gin have also resulted in a major contribution to medical knowledge, helping to fight serious diseases. Over the centuries, voyages undertaken by Royal Navy vessels often lasted months or even years. During these voyages, the availability of fresh food was limited to whatever could be carried on board or sourced at ports along the way. It was not unknown for crews to have to go on 'short rations' during a voyage, especially when bad weather prevented the vessel from reaching a port. The lack of fresh food meant that sailors suffered from scurvy, caused by lack of Vitamin C. This was a very serious disease, causing more deaths at sea than storms, shipwrecks, combat and other diseases. Historians have estimated that over 2 million sailors, whether serving in naval or trading ships, died from scurvy between the sixteenth and nineteenth centuries. Governments and ship owners expected to have approximately 50 per cent of a vessel's crew die from scurvy on every voyage.

Although there were many unsuccessful attempts to find solutions to the disease, it was not until 1747 that James Lind, a Scottish physician serving on board HMS *Salisbury*, found an answer. He had been carrying out a controlled experiment. Twelve sailors suffering from scurvy were divided into six pairs. All twelve sailors ate the same food and lived in the same quarters, but each pair was given a different treatment from the various cures being put forward to deal with scurvy. These included: a quart of hard cider; 25 drops of elixir of vitriol (diluted sulphuric acid); 2 spoonfuls of vinegar and half a pint of sea water; two oranges and one lemon; an electuary (a mix of garlic, mustard seed, balsam of Peru, dried radish root, gum myrrh); barley water treated with tamarinds and a laxative dose of cream of tartar. Five of the treatments were administered for fourteen days, but the citrus fruit could only be administered for seven days due to the fact that supplies ran out. Despite this, the men treated with citrus fruits recovered so quickly that they helped Lind care for the other sailors.

British sailors soon began to be known as 'limeys' due to their use of lemon and lime juice. But such fruit juice is very bitter and unpleasant to drink. The Royal Navy found an answer; Rear Admiral Sir Desmond Gimlette mixed gin (designed to fortify) and Rose's lime cordial (to protect from scurvy) to create a palatable drink. In due course, this combination became known as the Gimlet, a cocktail which is still mixed today. The name may also reflect the use of a gimlet corkscrew used on board to open gin barrels.

The Royal Navy was also involved in the creation of another well-loved combination, the gin and tonic. Malaria is a disease endemic throughout much of the world, being spread by mosquitos. Symptoms include fever, tiredness, vomiting and headaches, and it can result in anaemia, coma, and even death. Quinine was an accepted remedy, having been originally discovered by the Quechua Indians in Peru. They ground the bark of the cinchona tree into a fine powder and added it to liquid, in order to ease muscle spasms and fever. Brother Agostino Salumbrino, an apothecary, saw the Incas using quinine to treat fevers and sent a sample back to Rome to see if it could be used to treat malaria. Experiments proved successful and by 1768, the Royal Naval physician James Lind ordered that 'every man receive a daily ration of cinchona powder' whenever a naval vessel was anchored in a tropical port. The biggest problem was obtaining sufficient supplies of the cinchona bark, which was expensive and unreliable. By the 1840s, demand from soldiers and colonists in India had risen to over 700 tonnes of cinchona bark annually, and attempts were being made to find new sources of supply. Eventually, an expedition managed to obtain cinchona seeds and plants from the Andes. These seeds and plants were planted in India, Ceylon and in the Dutch East Indies.

With the opening up of new sources of cinchona, attention switched to ways of making it more palatable. It was normal practice to dissolve quinine in water and require malaria patients to drink it. Unfortunately this tonic water, as it became known, tasted horrible. The Royal Navy and the army in India began adding gin, lemon juice and using carbonated water to make it easier to drink. This led ultimately to the launch of Schweppes Indian Tonic Water combining lemon, water and quinine in a bottle ready to be served, without any need to first dissolve the quinine. According to Winston Churchill, 'the gin and tonic saved more Englishmen's lives, and minds, than all the doctors in the Empire.'

There were some undesirable results from this focus on quinine. In 1857, a new disease appeared – cinchonism, which caused sight loss, tinnitus and nausea resulting from drinking too much quinine. Instances of this disease are now rare, but still occasionally occur. In the 1970s, doctors diagnosed TV chef Clarissa Dickson Wright as suffering from malaria, but in reality she was experiencing quinine poisoning resulting from her long held habit of drinking two bottles of gin daily, accompanied with four pints of tonic water. The levels of quinine had built up in her body until she eventually began exhibiting signs of poisoning.

Modern-day tonics do not contain enough quinine to combat malaria. Patients would have to drink very large quantities of the manufactured tonic water in order to benefit from any anti-malarial properties. Having said that, tonic water is still sometimes used as a 'pick me up' to help symptoms of arthritis, coughs and colds due to its muscle relaxing properties as well as being a way of reducing high temperatures.

Gin-based cocktails have become a staple of naval life. The Pink Gin first appeared during the nineteenth century when sailors used Angostura bitters to help settle stomachs while at sea. To make the Angostura bitters taste better, they mixed it with rations of gin. In doing so, it turned the gin pink. In due course, Pink Gin became popular on land as well as at sea. This cocktail is even mentioned in *The Cruel Sea*, one of the most famous Second World War naval stories, dealing with naval ships sailing across the Atlantic. Author Nicholas Monserrat refers to the characters Lockhart and Ericson ordering Pink Gins when they met up in London.

Maritime links remain strong within the gin industry and will undoubtedly continue. Countless gins throughout the world are described as navy strength, or have maritime names. In Thailand a gin brand uses bottles that hark back to maritime use. Iron Balls gin uses small, stout bottles each with a wide flat bottom – a traditional style designed to enable bottles to stay upright on ships. It also links to the gin company founder's interest in exploring reefs and shipwrecks. The bottle design is not the only unusual aspect of this company. It was the first to be granted a distilling licence in Thailand for over thirty years, and its company motto includes the words, 'you always have options if you have balls'. The gin itself is made using large quantities of pineapples and coconuts.

In 2020, P&O Cruises launched the first gin to be produced in a distillery located on a cruise liner. The distillery is regarded as being a stand-out attraction on P&O *Iona* liner, being named after Columba, the sixth-century founder of the abbey on Iona. Branded as Marabelle, meaning Star of the Sea, the botanicals used include kelp to give a subtle hint of the sea. It has been created with the help of Angus Lugsdin, of the Salcombe Distilling company who says:

> Iona and the sea have been the inspiration for every element of Marabelle Gin, from the name and the design of the bottle label, with the star formations in the night sky overhead, to the flora native to the island of Iona, juniper and heather used in the recipe. The bottle label is in the shape of a gin pennant flag, a symbol of hospitality flown by sailors for years.

Chapter 9

Gin's New Dawn

As the twentieth century came to an end, a resurgence of interest in gin began to appear. The highly popular TV series, *Sex and the City*, featured a character called Carrie Bradshaw who frequently ordered Cosmopolitan cocktails: 'I'd like a cheese burger, large fries and a Cosmopolitan.' As a result, the Cosmopolitan (made with gin, cranberry juice, lime juice and Cointreau) quickly became the quintessential cocktail for fashionistas. The *New York* magazine reported the arrival of the 'cocktail culture'. Elaborate cocktails became fashionable, while retro favourites like Singapore Sling and Gimlets were drunk in ever-increasing quantities. Cocktails became de rigueur when out for a night on the town. Younger drinkers wanted authentic tastes and sought out premium gins like Hendrick's, Bombay Sapphire and Tanqueray No 10.

As sales of Hendrick's steadily climbed, owner Charlie Gordon's instinct had been proved right. Master Distiller, Lesley Gracie explains.

> In 1999 Charlie decided that we were to develop a new gin. At that point, nobody in the industry saw a potential market for gin, but Charlie thought the time was right and wanted to be in at the beginning. He wanted it made in a very specific way, using two different stills to create a very distinct flavour profile, lots of botanical notes and final notes of roses and cucumber.

Rise of the artisan gin distilleries

Gin was becoming fashionable again, yet London, once very much the capital of gin, still had few gin distilleries. That fact had not escaped attention. Over in America, the market for craft drinks, especially beer and gin, was expanding rapidly. Returning to the UK, Sam Galsworthy wondered why this was not happening in London where gin was traditionally known ad the 'Spirit of London'. There was a total lack of craft distilleries in the area. Research quickly identified the reason for this – an Act of Parliament dating back over 250 years. The Gin Act of 1751 had outlawed the creation of small-scale distilleries within London. It took two years for Galsworthy to persuade trade organisations and MPs to agree to the repealing of the Act. In 2008, the Gin Act was finally repealed. Just one year later, Galsworthy set up Sipsmith, the first small distillery in London since 1820.

The results were dramatic. Other craft distilleries quickly followed suit, sales of gin increased, leading to a revival of interest throughout the UK and fuelling gin's renaissance. In 2016, the *Telegraph* wrote 'The rise of British gin was boosted in 2009, when Sipsmith, based in West London, won a two-year legal battle with HMRC for the right to produce gin in small quantities rather than on an industrial scale.' The same year, 2016, also saw Sipsmith actually running out of gin due to the sheer scale of demand, and the following year over 30,000 visitors toured its distillery. Alongside this revival in craft gins was a growth in premium tonic waters such as Fever-Tree, providing a more authentic taste.

A BBC comedy series, *Fleabag*, included a priest character who had a liking for gin and tonic. Nor was it any gin and tonic, but it had to be 'cans of gin and tonic from Marks & Spencer'. When offered a can from a secret stash kept in the church sacristy, he described it as a 'proper drink'. Throughout the series, romance blossomed over the cans of gin and tonic. The resultant sales were high. Sales of the M&S gin and tonic cans rose sharply by 24 per cent after just one episode in April 2019. Marks & Spencer commented that 'This isn't any G&T in a can, it's a M&S G&T in a can ... an absolute favourite with M&S customers as well as the occasional vicar as seen recently on the hit show *Fleabag*.'

New gins began appearing on a regular basis, including novelties such as a gin incorporating a stick of Blackpool Rock. The range of flavours on offer became increasingly wide, introducing exotic as well as familiar flavours. Spotting an interest in nostalgic flavours led Raisthorpe Hall Distillery to create versions hinting at Lemon Drizzle Cake and Shimmering Bubble Gum. Even the surplus produce is being put to use. Raisthorpe is turning its surplus gin-soaked fruit into jam, while in Australia, leftover botanicals from the gin distillation process are used to make gin soaps and beard oils.

One of the strangest aspects of the gin renaissance that has taken place during the twenty-first century is the fact that it remains an industry dominated by males. Although women are among the biggest gin drinkers, the number of female gin distillers and brand owners is relatively low. Prominent among their numbers is Leslie Gracie, master distiller at Hendrick's, who has been involved from the beginning when she was asked to create a gin with a difference. Her innovative style has been maintained with experimental gins that include quinine-based gins formulated in a Victorian-style building known as Hendrick's Gin Palace, complete with its own greenhouses catering for plants growing in Mediterranean or a tropical climate. As the industry has developed, women have begun to set up their own brands, such as Kathy Caton's Brighton Gin and the Isle of Cumbrae distillery, which is owned by five women, one of whom is Canadian and another American. All five participants chose to train as the company distillers.

Revival of cocktails

Cocktails, too, have been revitalised due to the introduction of canned versions. Instead of having to wait for a bar tender, or buy numerous bottles and mixing equipment, drinkers can simply buy a pre-mixed cocktail, open the can, pour and drink. As Paul Bungener from Fair points out:

People come out of an office, they grab a bottle or buy a cocktail, sit in a park and enjoy a nice ambiance over the summer. People don't want to be bothered, they just want to fill up a glass and relax. Covid increased this trend – instead of waiting for a bartender to use several bottles with the possible health risks, the bar tender can just grab a pre-mixed bottle and bring it straight to the table. This reduces the risks. Since February 2020, sales of pre-mixed cocktails have increased in England, Germany, France and all the leading markets.

Strange cocktail events began to take place. In London, the Mad Hatter and Alice in Wonderland joined forces with Boë Gin to create a series of pop up Mad Hatter gin parties. Participants spent an evening disappearing down a rabbit hole into an immersive cocktail event hosted by a group of mad Alice in Wonderland characters. Guests were given a small bottle of red alcoholic liquid entitled 'Drink Me' and encountering Inhale-able Victoria Sponge. Screams of 'off with their heads' from the Queen of Hearts resulted in guests tumbling down the rabbit hole to take part in a psychedelic show involving mad party games and making cocktails, while drinking gin, gin and more gin. Smashing a meringue dessert enabled them to find a key to save the Knave from the Queen of Hearts.

Elsewhere, keen cocktail drinkers explored the strange and curious Jules Verne-style world in the fictional adventurer Phileas Fogg's idiosyncratic, Victorian-style gin parlour. At Mr Fogg's Society of Exploration they are invited to 'indulge in our exquisite and substantial selection of fine libations'. There are opportunities to 'encounter all means of exploration as you bear witness to the fruits of British industrial revolution in the form of new-fangled machinery and the bold experimentations of mixology within The Society of Exploration.'

In Hampshire, Highclere Castle is often described as 'the finest occupied Victorian mansion in England' and was the location for the iconic Downton Abbey TV series. This aristocratic country house imagery helped create the ambiance for an upmarket Highclere Gin, distilled by a local company in one of the oldest working copper gin stills dating back to the 1800s and made with juniper that has grown on the estate since Roman times. Drinkers are encouraged to imbibe it 'Highclere style' with tonic, orange juice, peel and a sprig of fresh rosemary. It also created 'A Butler's Guide to English cocktails' in which the Head Butler explained how to make classic cocktails. As Lady Carnarvon explains, 'cocktails, gin and Highclere are the perfect combination since the castle is renowned for entertaining and hosting weekend parties over gin cocktails going back ages.'

Nor has this latest gin revival been confined to the actual drinking of gin. Chefs are using gin in cooking, there are gin-based Christmas Puddings, gin sweets, gin drink doormats, gin popcorn, gin lip balms, gin-filled Christmas baubles complete with edible gold, and gin-related cards, such as a Valentine's Day card saying 'You're the gin to my tonic'. Even Nestlé, one of the biggest chocolate manufacturers, launched a special gin and tonic mint fondant flavour combination for its iconic After Eight Chocolates. Debbie Bowen, senior brand manager for After Eight says 'Gin has rapidly become the nation's spirit of choice, so what could be better than combining the flavours of our favourite tipple with the delicious mint fondant and dark chocolate that has made After Eight so popular for almost sixty years.'

Creating a gin brand has also become a favourite way of raising funds for charity. Examples can be found worldwide, covering every type of charitable organisation including conservation, heritage, sustainability, hospices and expeditions or simply a way of raising funds for a personal charity challenge such as completing a John O'Groats to Land's End event.

The reinvention of gin is complete – from a world of society cocktail drinkers to a world of mass-produced and craft gins and related products, gin has regained its prime position. The Wine and Spirit Trade Association reported that over 82 million bottles were sold in the UK during 2019, with UK gin sales surpassing £2bn for the first time. Sales continue to rise steadily, even during the Covid-19 pandemic, with online sales of gin being reported to have exceeded expectations. The UK has become the world's largest exporter of gin, with creativity and interest in gin being experienced worldwide.

Gin names

Looking to the past for inspiration is common among modern gin brands, as they find the darker side of gin's history stimulating and creative, using names such as Rogue Society Gin and Scrapegrace Goldilocks. The past has provided not just a constant source of ideas for brand names but also packaging and marketing initiatives highlighting the darker side of gin's heritage including illicit gin, war, death and secret societies. The advertising of gin has incurred considerable controversy, with companies always having to tread a careful line between promoting a desirable product, and not encouraging people to drink too much.

For centuries, gin was rarely given a specific name nor was it branded or have distinctive packaging. It came in barrels, simply as gin or genever direct from the distiller. Customers simply asked for a 'pennyworth of gin' or provided a tankard in which to place the drink. Even today, it is still common for drinkers to ask for a 'gin and tonic' without specifying a brand name. This is due to the fact that until a few years ago, the average pub, wine bar or restaurant would have served just one gin and one brand of tonic – the brands supplied by their brewer, pubco or wholesaler.

The idea of giving various types of gin names first emerged during the eighteenth century, at a time when heavy drinking was the norm. These were very descriptive and easily memorable names such as 'Cream of the Valley' and 'Celebrated Butter Gin'. Since most of the drinkers would probably have been illiterate, such names would have helped them quickly identify exactly what they wanted, rather than reflecting the actual taste. It also made the drinks more aspirational since most paupers were unlikely to be able to afford butter, instead having to be content with far cheaper spreads like beef dripping.

Old Tom is one of the best-known gin names, and can be found worldwide. Countless distillers have developed their own version of Old Tom gin. The origins of the name go back hundreds of years into gin's dark and murky past. Traditionally, Old Tom was a slightly sweeter, less botanical type of gin. Some people believe that Old Tom may have got its name from a poor old tom cat drowning in a vat of gin. Others say that Old Tom is linked to the cat image in Captain Dudley Bradstreet's innovative wall-mounted gin vending system. Yet another story links Old Tom to a distiller called Thomas Chamberlain and his apprentice, Thomas Norris, both of whom worked at Hodge's Distillery, London. When Norris (young Tom) finished his apprenticeship, he opened a gin palace at Great Russell Street, Covent Garden. The gin on sale was called Old Tom in honour of Thomas Chamberlain, and marked with this name on the barrels. The first trademarked Old Tom appeared in 1849, when Joseph Boord created an Old Tom brand.

During the early twentieth century, Old Tom had been the lynchpin of many cocktails, especially in America. Prohibition reduced the demand and by the 1950s, Old Tom Gin styles had almost disappeared. The resurgence in interest in gin and cocktails led to its reappearance when Hayman Distillers revived a family recipe dating back to 1870. Since then, there have been countless new Old Tom gins being launched from as far afield as Sweden, Australia and Glasgow.

Although the exact origins of Old Tom lie hidden in the past, what is certain is that Old Tom gins have been drunk for a very long time and that some of the versions were very questionable. Low quality gin was often masked by strong flavours of sugar, liquorice and even adulterated with substances like turpentine. Nowadays, Old Tom gins are much higher quality. York Gin's Old Tom is now recognised as one of the world's finest, and was devised as part of a collaboration with a Michelin-starred restaurant.

Recipes and names from the past have frequently prompted companies to create gin brands. Hammer & Co. developed an Old English Gin made from a 1783 recipe, distilling eleven botanicals within one of the oldest pots still in existence. Adding to the historic ambiance, the gin is presented in silk-printed champagne bottles direct from a barrel as a Barman's Special Reserve since the company wanted to reinvigorate the way in which English gin was made and served at the time. At Portobello Road Gin, a Victorian name 'Celebrated Butter Gin' was revived to create a gin for the twenty-first century. Commenting that the original name was probably a marketing tool to give the impression that the gin was high quality since sugar and butter would have too expensive for most people, their version was created by redistilling its classic Portobello Road Gin with ten blocks of English unsalted butter giving it a creamy mouthfeel. Portobello Road's recipe master, Jake Burger, described the resultant Celebrated Butter Gin as being 'like meeting your friend's twin without knowing they had one, catching you unawares, and befuddling one's expectations in a thoroughly welcoming turn.'

The historical impact of Prohibition has led to the terms 'moonshine' and 'bathtub gin'. Numerous gin companies around the world incorporate the term bathtub gin within their ranges or utilise the Prohibition concept. Manchester-based O'Donnell Moonshine links its products directly into the Prohibition era when US farmers named their bootleg drink 'moonshine' putting it into preserving jars (Mason Jars) as these were easier to obtain in legitimate quantities than a more conventional drinks bottle. The company's namesake is Edward 'Spike' O'Donnell, leader of the South Side O'Donnell gang during the 1920s' bootleg wars in Chicago, who had few scruples when it came to fighting with other gangsters but insisted on a quality moonshine drink. Inspired by this story, O'Donnell Moonshine set out to bring this disreputable drink back to life. The resultant product is handcrafted and bottled in authentic Mason Jars, just like those used by the 1920s bootleggers.

The marketing of gin brands

In Edinburgh, Pickering's Gin is owned by two friends who have a background in engineering, furniture restoration and property renovation. The company has developed a reputation for being different, and idiosyncratic combining history and quirky inventiveness. The premises are an old dog kennels, which they decided to convert into a distillery simply because they liked gin, and had just inherited a gin recipe dating back to 1947. Their attitude is very simple: 'If you can't find what you want, make it yourself'. They rolled up their sleeves and built a distillery, then tried, tested and experiment until they were experts and had tailored their original recipe to suit modern tastes. The original recipe was based on a Bombay recipe, full of fragrant spices and fresh citrus fruits, but required adjusting to create a softer, smoother style of gin. In order to achieve this, they engineered a bain-marie heating system for the 500-litre copper stills enabling the botanicals to enjoy a slow luxurious simmer during distillation. This was the start of the 'botanical engineers'. Pickering's continues to innovate, developing everything from gin baubles to quirky vehicles designed to make people smile. It also ensures that the company is extremely memorable. Their inventions are certainly different.

The Tip Top Tippling Trunk is described as the essential kit for a botanical engineer combined with gin salesman. An old trunk languishing in a flea shop was adapted to contain all the paraphernalia of gin tasting, including three bottles of Pickering's Gin, lights, music and stickers from their travels. Then there is the Marvellously Mixed Musical Martini Maker Mark II. The original version was made from a wind-up gramophone found in India, a 1940s' American lamp, chemistry equipment dating from the 1960s and a coffee cafetière found in a local charity shop. This version now occupies a prominent position within the company's bar in Beijing, China and mixes drinks at 78rpm. The latest model to be found in the company headquarters has been fitted with lights and a catalogue of over 1,000 records.

A 650cc 4WD Daihatsu Hi-Jet Japanese Airport fire engine was purchased via eBay and taken to Edinburgh to be re-engineered as a Thirst Extinguisher dispensing gin through its hoses. Six different cocktails are dispensed from the pressurised canisters on the sides, through the hoses, straight into glasses, making it a perfect, eye-catching addition to any promotional event. They believe that their Monkeybike is probably the smallest mobile gin bar in the world. Purchased from a neighbouring company for two bottles of gin, they stripped it down, restored each part and painted her. An old leather box was added together with bits of an old coffee table, a plumbing kit and lab equipment.

Even the simple matter of putting on bottle labels resulted in an innovative solution in the form of Mabel the labeller. Pickering's Gin bottles are heavy to hold, square with curved edges and gently tapered. As the company point out, 'a bugger to wrap a label around. Change the bottle? Not a bit of it. We invented our own machine to affix the labels perfectly every time. She was only meant to label batch one. She managed 100,000 bottles of Pickering's Gin before we retired her in 2016.' Their gin range is just as memorable including tastes such as Brussels Sprout Gin, Forget-me-not Gin and Gingerbread Gin.

Hendrick's Gin takes a very idiosyncratic, curious approach to its marketing, positioning itself as whimsical, entertaining, slightly mock-Victorian in its approach. In November 2020, it launched its first ever TV advert involving a short animated fantasy film embodying Victorian surrealism, inviting gin drinkers to heed the call of their curiosity. The distinctive film depicts a butler, who also happens to be a hammerhead shark, at his daily tasks. Intrigued by a Martini glass-shaped crack in the wall, his curiosity helps him deliver the secret magical world of Hendrick's Gin complete with tiny fairy like ballet dancers. The voiceover invites viewers to:

Leave the mundane, heed the call of your curiosity,
Escape the conventional and embrace the Delectable

Welcome to the world of Hendrick's Gin
Undeniably peculiar, utterly delicious.

The advert was created by Quaker City Mercantile whose director Jerry Stifelmann comments: 'this advert is simply an allegory for our gin. With its infusions of rose and cucumber, Hendrick's at first seems unusual – yet when you investigate further by taking a sip, you discover a delectable world of wondrous flavour.'

Over in Australia, Hendrick's Gin continued its unconventional approach by offering drinkers in Sydney free rides in its one-of-a-kind gin balloon bar reaching over 30 metres from the ground while sipping on a gin Martini. Luke Sanderson, Brand Ambassador of Hendrick's Gin said:

It's not a Hendrick's Gin affair without the extraordinary. We have gone above and beyond to bring Sydneysiders a spectacle from the street to the sky in the most unusual style. Adding whimsy and wonder is what we do. We hope Sydneysiders will join our celebration of the unusual and raise a glass to celebrate a summer like none other.

Brand images used by gin companies can have quite dark connotations. Gordon's Gin contains the image of a ferocious boar's head on the bottle cap. It refers to a legend that a member of the Gordon clan once saved the king of Scotland from a wild boar while out hunting. The Gordon clan has always had the boar's head on its coat of arms and uses it as a trademark on its gin. Other gin brands have included Felons Gin, Beware of the Woods, and Rogue Cooler. Fire combined with conservation requirements created an unusual Yorkshire-based gin known as Smouldering Heights Gin. This concept was inspired by the annual heather burning which takes place on the Yorkshire moors in order to encourage new plant growth providing food for sheep and grouse. The result is a gin with an earthy smoky background derived from peat-smoked malt, heather and Szechuan pepper.

Set up in the midst of the Covid-19 pandemic, Gyre & Gimble Gin Company chose to reflect the strange world in which they found themselves by linking with Alice in Wonderland, the most iconic crazy, dark story. The result was a range of gins such as the Queen of Hearts, Callooh Callay and Nowhow with labels bearing Alice themes like the Walrus and oysters.

Equally unusual is the approach taken by the County Durham-based Herbal Gin Company. It incorporates innovative marketing techniques to attract the attention of gin drinkers as the company's Aviator Gin Bar features a full size helicopter complete with a disco ball. Owners Colin Scott and Wayne Richardson purchased the huge Eurocopter for six bottles of gin, when the helicopter was being retired after three decades in service. The quirky bar includes tables and chairs from salvaged holiday jets while seating pods are made from salvaged parts of Airbus A340s and a Boeing 737.

Ever since the eighteenth century, gin has possessed illicit connotations whether through illicit distilling, through smuggling or through links to crime and violence. Darran Edmond, founder of the Illicit Spirits Distillery in Glasgow felt that such illicit connotations would work well for his company helping it stand out with an instantly memorable name. Operating from urban premises located under a railway arch, the underground references combined perfectly with the dark history of gin. A further link was the use of small-batch distilling using copper stills which can be quickly be dismantled – a feature that would have been extremely important to the illicit distillers hundreds of years ago as they needed to be able to move their equipment quickly when revenue inspectors were in the area. As Darran acknowledges, the name did cause some problems when setting up the business, particularly when dealing with HM Revenue & Customs. The use of the term 'Illicit' in registering the company resulted in emails often being rejected, being flagged up as a problem company. It has even caused problems for potential customers accessing the website from business premises as some systems flag up the word illicit and refuse requests to allow access to the site. Darran comments:

> Almost every perceived weakness in business can be played to your advantage. Illicit distilling was obviously massive in Scotland centuries ago and the whisky that was being produced by the illicit guys on their little pot stills had a much better reputation than the stuff that was made on a large scale. So hopefully our small-batch spirits produced under the railway arches is of high quality.

Illicit Spirits seek to combine the creation of innovative spirits with traditional methods used by the illicit distillers of old. Just like those distillers of past years, they create small batches of gin in copper pot stills. Labels reinforce this period ambiance incorporating Hogarthian images while the gin styles are equally linked to the past. Even the description of their Blacklist Smoked Gin carries historical references: 'They gave me some cursed stuff they called gin – such blasphemy I never heard … this was the unChristianest, beastliest liquor I ever tasted.' If a brew was too dark, it could be blacklisted for being the wrong shade. Smoking juniper berries over Scottish peat gives the beverage a deep smoky flavour, which is complemented by black cardamoms, black peppercorns, lapsang souchong tea and activated charcoal to create an unconventional gin. The resultant gin is truly black and dark resulting from the way in which peat smoke is bubbled through the gin.

At the same time, the Illicit Spirits Distillery has sought to use historic elements within its branding by utilising eighteenth-century Hogarth style images superimposed with the company's logo, creating a clash between the modern and traditional. As Darran explains 'From the outset, it has been our philosophy to look to the past – but with a critical eye, without reverence or nostalgia – taking the best from history and finding a way to interpret tradition in a way that's interesting or unexpected.'

Some brands are created by accident. Taking on some run down old properties in Palmers Green, London with the intention of converting them into offices for his plumbing company unexpectedly resulted in the owner becoming involved in gin distilling based on a Victorian illicit recipe. Ian Puddick explains:

> I had to remove an old building chimney on the property as trees were growing up the middle and making it unsafe. I got sued by my neighbour, who claimed ownership of the chimney and it came down to questions of provenance. The lawyers told me to see if I could find any illustrations showing that it was part of the site over 100 years ago during the 1860–1880 period. I tracked down the people who owned the site at that time, and managed to find an old picture showing the chimney as well as finding out more about the business operating in the buildings at that time.

The site was known as the Old Bakery and as he discovered, they had provided more than just bread.

> They were an East End family, making illicit gin. The size of the ovens showed that they were providing bread on a large scale and doing other things. Gin was sold at a cash price. It was a crime family, doing a lot of back of the lorry type of trading and at one point were doing a massive trade in stolen paint with great sheds of the stuff. Their descendants were embarrassed about it, and while they didn't give me a recipe, they did say that the gin had been made using four botanicals one of which was juniper.

One family member suggested that stinging nettles might have been involved.

Along with his dad – a retired soldier and intelligence officer - gin fan Ian Puddick just had to experiment. As he points out, 'A hundred years ago they made illegal gin in my office. You couldn't make that up. So I had to try to make gin.'

Turning to YouTube for help, they began playing around with distilling methods and the botanicals to get a decent taste. Stinging nettles were not included, since 'the taste was awful'. Setting up a small distillery complete with the words 'Illicit Gin sold here', they created a subsidiary business making gin, targeting the top end of the market. Sales grew steadily, with supplies often being delivered to Fortnum & Mason's using Puddick's plumbers' van. 'We went to Junipalooza [a major gin exhibition] and turned out to be the biggest selling gin in the show,' Puddick recalled. 'Two weeks later, we had the marketing director and CEO of Pernod Ricard come to see us because they hadn't been able to get anywhere near our stand at the show. There had been too many people around it. We had people from Spain and Germany visit us and the offer of a £1m contract from Lidl – we turned it down.'

The Old Bakery Gin aroused yet more controversy locally during the renovations. While rebuilding a wall within the mews, Puddick began chatting to an elderly man who lived in one of the houses opposite to the wall.

> He was 103 years old, and had lived in the house all his life. He remembered the building when it was a bakery and asked if we were going to put the sign back. We knew nothing about this as there were no traces left. He showed me an old photograph and I studied it carefully, counted up all the bricks top to bottom, the width to give the exact dimensions and size of the letters. We reinstated the original sign using a sign writer who was used to restoring ghost signs.

He continued:

> Two and a half months later, the council got in touch and told us to remove the graffiti on our wall. They gave me

fourteen days to do it or they would do it for us. They put an enforcement notice on it. I wrote to them and appealed, pointing out that we had pictures of the original sign in place. They rejected our appeal. I went to the local councillor and he came over and studied it. We stood in the road, drinking mugs of tea and looking at it as I told him the story. He kept saying, 'I love it.' He went to the council department involved, had the enforcement notice revoked and made them list it. The sign is now a listed heritage monument. You couldn't make it up!

The story behind this unusual gin company made the news, resulting in an appearance on television. Former Tory government minister and now TV broadcaster Michael Portillo visited the distillery in 2017, as part of one of his railway programmes. He was filmed looking at and standing beside the illicit gin sign within the distillery. Portillo commented that 'the story puts a spell on you'.

Packaging gin

Heritage has also provided inspiration for packaging. In Scotland, glass company Angels' Share Glass decided to resurrect unusual nineteenth-century gin pig decanters. During the nineteenth century, there was a trend for wealthy households to have specially made decanters for use with individual types of alcohol. At Brodie Castle, Moray (now in the care of the National Trust for Scotland), there was a tradition of using gin pigs. The clear decanter is picked up by the pig's tail and the drink poured out through the pig's nose, which is marked by a cork stopper.

Purchasers of the German Archaeologist Gin are more likely to be interested in the bottle rather than the gin itself. Developed by Uwe Ehinger, the Archaeologist Gin is a combination of Uwe's two interests: gin and motorbikes. A custom-made motorcycle builder,

Uwe has spent many years tracking down old motorbikes around the world, especially Harley Davidsons. Every bottle of Archaeologist Gin is unique, as the contents include a rare motorbike part chosen at random from Uwe's collection. Each motorbike part is sealed in a tin to provide contaminating the gin, and can range from a 1939 Flathead camshaft found in the Mexican desert to a 1962 Panhead rocker arm discovered in South Korea. The bottles are then packaged using historic map illustrations printed on an original Heidelberg Tiegel printing press dating from 1931. Obtaining a bottle of this rare gin is not easy, as production is extremely limited and very expensive. Each bottle costs over $1,000 and sells out as soon as it is released. There is a long waiting list.

Stories of fallen angels can be found in every culture around the world. These are angels no longer allowed to live in heaven, angels who have sinned or tempt humans to sin. Fallen Angels appear in literature like Dante Aligheri's Divine Comedy, or John Milton's Paradise Lost. The idea struck a chord when James Taylor was seeking to create a gin brand with a difference. He comments:

I asked myself why does a bottle have to look like a traditional conventional bottle? I saw the crystal skull used by Benson & Hedges in their South African advertising campaign and through it was a good idea. I was listening to a book by Arthur C. Clarke entitled *Guardian Angel* set in a post-cold war UK, complete with echoes of Roswell and Aliens. In that story, an alien overlord takes over, looking a little like the devil. The image of the devil, the fallen angel, is found everywhere in the world. It was a wonderful image and stayed in my mind. I wondered if it would be possible to make a bottle that looked like the devil, which would be instantly recognisable everywhere in the world. It is the bottle which makes a gin memorable and stands out.

Taylor searched throughout Europe to find a company who could make the type of bottle he wanted, and finally found a glass company in Slovenia. The resultant iconic glass bottles have now become collectors' items, with people turning them into lamps, lanterns, and vases. Candles placed inside create an eerie glow. Other versions included a hand-painted design incorporating the Four Horsemen of the Apocalypse. The design attracted attention and he was approached by a business from Stoke-on-Trent keen to make a ceramic version, which has proved equally popular with people wanting a premium product, and led him to work on other dark themes such as Medusa, whose gaze turned people into stone. He added:

> People like the idea of a fallen angel, they want to be an anti-hero, because they know they are not perfect. Fallen Angel gins are supercharged, intense full on tastes, reflecting the bottle as well as my own personality. The blends are relevant to the image. Blood Orange is reddish in colour and we mix Seville oranges to make it less astringent.

Twisted gins have become a feature of the Gin Renaissance, the rebirth of gin that has taken place over the first two decades of the twenty-first century. Afterthought Gin is a specialist in this sector, featuring bottles that are twisted soda bottles from the 1930s. The term has come to have a dual meaning with both the twist in the bottle and the way Afterthought were twisting different botanicals together in the laboratory while creating a gin. Doug Walford, one of the founders, commented:

> We wanted to do something different and use a ceramic bottle. We contacted a Stoke on Trent ceramics company with the idea of a ceramic bottle with a twist in it. They experimented with it, and developed a three piece mould. When people see the bottle, it is like "Wow, it's amazing". It was an expensive

and difficult process, but worth it because it attracts attention, and helps us be memorable in a saturated market. We are very big on vapour infusion, and our method involves a basic gin recipe with ten botanicals and then we twist with additional botanicals then we twist to make it different.

A legacy of secret societies dating back over a hundred years was used as the inspiration for the launch of the first ever Chinese gin brand. Known as Peddlers Gin, it is produced in the same style of apothecary style bottles that would have been used by street sellers in the early twentieth century. Bartenders in China were sent an antique key in an enveloped sealed with wax and stamped with the Peddlers logo. A week later, the top 100 bar tenders received a special mah-jong box. They had to use the key to unlock the box to reveal three mah-jong tiles. Lifting up the inner lid, they were faced with a variety of mah-jong symbols. Matching the tiles to the appropriate symbols led to the discovery of a secret trap door leading to a hidden bottle of gin. The bar tenders loved the secrecy and reminders of the dark, secret societies that are part of the Chinese heritage.

Turning to the past does not always work out quite as intended when it comes to marketing and selling. Railroad Events introduced a 'Gin Train' concept combining steam train heritage with an opportunity to try out various gins. Participants were told they could 'sip a sundowner aboard a vintage train while watching the countryside gently rolling by.' For travellers on the Mid Norfolk Line Gin Train, it turned into a nightmare due to a combination of a heatwave and poor service, resulting in many customers receiving far less gin than they had expected. Equally traumatic was the attempt to create gin festivals similar to the well-established network of beer festivals. Having sold over 20,000 advance tickets at venues across the UK, Gin Festival Limited collapsed and went into administration leaving distillers and consumers out of pocket.

Much more successful was the decision of marketeers at Beefeater Gin to use Jack the Ripper to highlight the brand's London connections.

The company ran a memorable 'London Calling' campaign involving voicemails on podcasts and Spotify aiming to entice participants into a London phone booth for a chat with Jack the Ripper or James Bond. The message stated:

> It's Jack the Ripper. Let's you and I tear up to town, figuratively speaking of course, (laughs) or go for a drink. Beefeaters London Dry Gin is the origin, good enough for a genuine Londoner like me. Give me a ring when you are back.

This is then followed by a female voice saying,

> Sometimes doing things the proper way involves a bit of risk. Find a Beefeaters Dry Gin phone booth in your city and call Jack back. Beefeaters Dry London Gin, it's proper London.

The campaign proved extremely memorable and popular, raising awareness of the brand worldwide due to the linking of such well-known images.

Tucked away in some of the most remote corners of Scotland are countless small bothies, once the home of shepherds but now acting as a place of refuge for weary hikers and climbers. Gin now plays a part in the Bothy Experience, a centre within the village of Glamis enabling visitors to discover the stories and heritage that lie behind the concept of 'bothying'. This is the venue for Bothy Gins, which are infused with seasonal produce from local berry fields and farms. The gins were created by accident as founder Kim Cameron initially set about making award winning jams. Her mother suggested using the residual fruit juice to make gin, and the resulting alcohol is based on a seventeenth-century recipe favoured by bothy dwellers. The Bothy Experience has become a place for people to linger and enjoy not just the gin, but the bothy culture and haunting bothy ballads, as Kim indicates:

We wanted to celebrate the culture and community around bothies – to keep them alive in our hearts and minds. They're a place where travellers converge as kindred spirits and hip flasks are passed around. They're a place of stories, a way of reconnecting with the past.

In Australia, the Death Gin Company has created an entire story line around its brand. The company's website poses an unusual question for its customers stating:

Now like every good spirit company, we've got an original tale that treads the line of fact and fantasy.

Did we make it up ourselves?
Did we plagiarise a Year 11 history textbook?
Did we pay someone a bottle of Death Gin to write it for us?
You be the judge.

Their story line is definitely inventive. Set on the outskirts of Rutherglen, on Distillery Road, there is a small graveyard. Hidden on the bark of a eucalyptus tree are the letters MM, marking the last resting place of bushranger Patrick Black.

The story goes that Distillery Road was named after an illegal still which operated there during the 1860s. Although discovered and partly destroyed by the local authorities, Black turned it into his hideout and reopened the still.

Declared an outlaw, Black stole from merchants and gave the spoils to local townsfolk. He also traded his gin with them, naming it Death Gin due to the fact that he had originally been an undertaker.

The story continues:

On 13 February 1875, Black was ambushed by the constabulary on the outskirts of Rutherglen. He managed a daring escape back to his hideout but as fate would have it, caught a single shot in his stomach. Apparently, Black was visited by a strange vagabond draped in rags and carrying a scythe. Black knew instantly that this was Death, come to take him over the threshold. Since Black had no next of kin or indeed anyone he could call a close friend, he asked one last favour of Death – to bury his body after he departed this world for the next. Having given away all his riches, Black offered Death his last earthly possession – a bottle of gin. Now Death wasn't accustomed to these sort of requests, but just because he didn't have a heart, didn't mean he was heartless. So Death agreed, and these two unlikely companions sat and drank and told tales until the first rays of sunrise touched the treetops and Black finally succumbed to his wounds.

As he had promised, Death buried Black under a gumtree behind a nearby graveyard and with his scythe scorched MM into the trunk. This stood for MOMENTO MORI – Black's motto in life … From that day onward, on the anniversary of Black's death, a mysterious veiled woman could be seen visiting the tree, carrying a bottle of gin. She would drink one single shot, in honour of the shot that took Black's life, and bury the rest for Black and Death to enjoy once again while telling tales until the sunrise hit the treetops.

So is this fiction or reality? Death Gin never says, leaving readers to make their own decisions.

As the number of gin brands has proliferated, arousing public awareness and recognition has become ever more important. Catchy slogans such as 'Bombay Sapphire. Pour something priceless'; 'Gilbey's Taste the Smoothest gin today. Good times last longer'; Gordon's 'Refreshing yet dry. Mix Gordon's with pleasure. Re-Mix yourself. Go for a Gordon's'; 'Ready to Tanqueray' tend to stay in the memory. Most gin bottles look alike when on the shelves of a supermarket or behind the bar in a pub, where quite often it is hard to actually read the names. Having a clearly identifiable label such as a Cheshire Cat or bottle colour such as Bombay Sapphire's iconic blue can make a difference in customer choice. In a world dominated by visual images, ways of ensuring that brands reach the public eye are constantly being sought. This may be through TV advertising, product promotions or by participation in TV shows.

Many gin companies have opted to appear on *Dragons' Den* as it offers prime time coverage as well as potential investment. Didsbury Gin's Liam Manton was quite open about their reasons for going on the programme – the opportunity of putting their product in front of a million people. However, such participation also brings risks – getting it wrong could equally destroy a company's reputation. Planning on providing the dragons with a drink of gin during the presentation, it was purely by chance that Manton and his colleague Mark Smallwood checked the glasses beforehand. Having washed the glasses in the sink, they discovered that the water was drawn from a rarely used water tank, and the glasses now smelt of rotten eggs. This would have immediately destroyed any chance of investment. Two minutes before going on screen, there was a frantic rush to boil water to clean the glasses. Didsbury Gin succeeded in gaining investment from dragon Jenny Campbell, and her business acumen has proved a valuable asset as Manton comments: 'we skirt through disaster at least three times a week, but somehow it's working.'

Controversial advertising

Over the past century, methods of advertising gin have become a common source of controversy. In 1903, Boord & Sons took court action to defend their trademark against Huddart & Company. Boord & Sons had been the first distiller to register the image of a cat on a barrel as a trademark for Old Tom Gin in 1849. Huddart & Company had sought to use a similar image, and was challenged by Boord's under the Passing Off laws. The resultant case became a landmark in UK trademark law. In the evidence placed before Mr Justice Swinfen Eady, Boords proved that the image of a cat on a barrel referred to a man 'formerly old Thomas Chamberlain of Hodge's Distillery'. The distiller, Thomas Norris, had named the gin in honour of his former employer. The evidence presented included original labels bearing the picture of Old Tom, stressing the fact that it referred to an actual person rather than the oft-quoted legend that the name came from an old tom cat who had fallen into a vat of gin.

Another company which found itself encountering gin trademark problems was Halewood International. It sought to register a Vera Lynn trademark for alcoholic drinks. Dame Vera Lynn, an iconic wartime singer, objected, saying that placing her name on alcoholic drinks could be regarded as product endorsement. Although Halewood claimed that their trademark was a reference to Cockney rhyming slang for gin, rather than Dame Vera Lynn herself, the courts disagreed and ruled in Dame Vera Lynn's favour.

Equally controversial was the decision by Brittany-based distillers Awen Nature to launch a Gin Ganesh. It immediately came under criticism from Hindu religious leaders on the basis that Gin Ganesh was named after a god and used Hindu symbols: a blue elephant resembling the Hindu god was used on the label. Religious leader Rajan Zed pointed out that Ganesh was meant to be worshipped and not promote a gin, commenting: 'Distilleries should not be in the business of religious appropriation, sacrilege and ridiculing entire communities. It was deeply trivialising of divine Hindu deity to be displayed on a gin bottle.'

A Nicholson Gin advert promoted itself as being 'too good to drown' using the image of an elephant blowing water over a bowler-hatted gentleman holding a glass of gin. During the 1960s, Booth's Gin issued an advertisement for its House of Lords Gin. It showed a brown tie, with the words 'Protest against the Rising Tide of conformity', plus a box containing the words 'I hate conformity because … ' (leaving space for an answer). Underneath the image were the words:

> Tell us your beef against society in 25 words or less [sic] and we won't send you this Booth's House of Lords Protest tie. Anyone can give you a premium offer. Booth's House of Lords gives you a really fine gin and a chance to shoot your mouth with absolutely no risk. All comments will be totally ignored. Not a chance of winning anything. Now that the competitive pressure is off, why not take advantage of this great opportunity? Do it today. Or next year. It really doesn't matter. There's no time limit on taking a stand against conformity. You'll never be inspired by a faddist gin. Instead try Booth's House of Lords. Have it on the rocks in a brand glass. We call it a Snifferini. But you can call it anything you like. That's one reason why many people regard Booth's as the non-conformist gin from England. Regardwise, it's the highest we can be held in.

In the 1970s, Gilbey's Gin was accused of being involved in subliminal advertising. Its controversial advertising campaign had experimented with subliminal advertising in an attempt to sell more bottles of gin. Images showed a bottle of gin beside a glass filled with liquid, with three ice cubes inside which were slightly shaped and appeared to have deeper, white markings on them. Researchers discovered that the markings on the ice cubes spelt the word 'sex'.

In 2019, Trossach Distillery broadcast a TV advert for its McQueen Gin. It featured three people walking in the Scottish Highlands, helping each other to reach the top of a craggy mountain while yet another scene showed a wetsuit-clad person diving into a loch. Each scene was interspersed by scenes of drinks being poured in which a glass of gin was garnished with ice, berries and lime. The advert ended with a shot of a gin bottle with the Scottish Highlands in the background, and the words 'McQueen – Adventurous Scottish Spirit #distilledtobedifferent.' An accompanying voiceover stated: 'Choose to explore; choose diving into something new; choose taking a different direction; choose nature and its elements; choose bringing your friends to the top; choose a drink full of adventure; choose McQueen Gin, adventurous Scottish spirit.'

Complaints to the UK Advertising Standards Authority (ASA) soon followed. The advertisement was subsequently banned on the basis that it linked alcohol consumption with mountain climbing. According to the ASA:

> The implication of the sequence of events shown in the ads was that the group drank McQueen Gin and a mixer at the summit of a mountain peak, after which they would need to make their way down: although sporting and physical activities are allowed in alcohol advertising, ASA states adverts must not imply that such activities have been carried out under the influence of alcohol.

Consequently, the ASA ruled that the advertisement breached the code.

Even more controversial was the promotional activity involved in launching a new gin for Bristol Dry Gin in June 2020, just as the Black Lives Matter campaign got underway. The company posted a tweet showing images of rioting plus the words, 'when the shooting starts the looting starts. Voted No. 1 gin by rioters for its complex botanical mix and high flammability. #gin # Bristol #PartyParott #burning bridges.' The words were also accompanied by a photo of bottles of their gin being prepared for use as a Molotov cocktail. The advert referenced a highly controversial Donald Trump tweet relating to the death of George Floyd in the USA. Bristol Dry Gin was widely criticised, and cafes and retailers removed the brand from sale. Tom Quarrelle, one of the landlords at the Plough in

Easton, commented that the pub would no longer stock Bristol Dry Gin adding, 'Sometimes it feels like our own real power is where we spend our money. Seeing a local company co-opting those words as an edgy joke to shock people and gain attention for their brand pissed me off.'

The company had to apologise for its 'insensitive tweet', saying that it was not a calculated publicity stunt. It claimed that it was a 'misjudged attempt to make a joke' and that they were genuinely sorry for causing offence. 'We were nothing other than devastated about the negative impact we had.' Bristol Dry Gin claimed it had not foreseen that its tweet would have 'such an impact' and that it had not dealt with the 'fallout' well, fearing it would make the situation worse. It admitted 'We got it badly wrong' and that the company had now contacted the Black Lives Matter and Stand Against Racism and Inequality with an offer to 'support its work'.

Drinkers and publicans were not convinced by the actions and apology of Bristol Dry Gin. Tom Quarrelle said:

> I think that the campaign was clickbait to generate controversy, traffic and ultimately sell more gin. They quoted Trump's rhetoric in response to the protests, to racism and the brutal killing of a black man as a marketing campaign. If you use shock tactics, be prepared for people to be shocked. It's not the first time they have courted controversy as a marketing strategy.

On an earlier occasion, Bristol Gin had launched a Novichok vodka in the same week that a mother of three died from the nerve agent, and other people were in intensive care from Novichok's effects. Other criticisms being made on social media included describing the company as a 'wannabee hipster edge lord', with gins poking fun at issues like murder, civil unrest, sexuality and homelessness. Their Turbo Island Gin was described as being 'tailored for the burgeoning homeless population of the city'. Bristol people also pointed to the fact that the company's 'About' page (subsequently deleted) had originally included the words 'our ideology is essentially that if more than twenty people tell you not to do something, and you think it is probably illegal, that doesn't necessarily mean that you shouldn't crack on and do it anyway. You can always issue an apology in the local paper.'

Gin proved the downfall for a team taking part in The Apprentice TV series during 2016. In the series, a group of aspiring young businessmen and women were competing for the chance to work with entrepreneur Lord Sugar, founder of the Amstrad electronics brand. In one of the challenges undertaken to test the various participants, teams were tasked with creating and releasing a gin. Team Titan opted to create an orange gin bearing the name Colony and incorporated a geographically incorrect map of the world on the label. Even before judging, their concept gin was widely attacked in the press and social media, branding it racist and celebrating colonialism. Lord Sugar criticised Team Titan for the concept's 'negative connotations' and prospective wine buyers were equally unenthusiastic ordering just £5,280-worth of gin compared to the opposing team's £71,400. Twitter critics commented: 'Colony Gin, this gin is made from the tears of slaves' and 'Orange, racist gin? Might not have got many orders but could potentially win a presidential election.' The Apprentice's own official Twitter account was equally damning referring to, 'A gin infused with artificial orange colouring that celebrates colonialism and features an incorrect map.'

Controversies about quality and strength

Reservations still surface about the quality of gin. In 2019, Hayman's Gin launched a campaign entitled 'Call Time on Fake Gin'. Questions were raised as to what exactly constituted gin, due to the increasing prevalence of gins laced with foodstuffs such as chocolate and fruit when regulations state that the main flavour of gin has to be juniper.

It was felt that some flavoured gins were misleading customers by blurring the boundaries.

Chris Bryant-Mansell, Brand Ambassador for Hayman's explains what had happened:

> The category was spiralling out of control with products labelled as 'gin' without meeting the basic requirements to be defined as gin:
>
> > Must be predominantly juniper flavoured
> > Must be over 37.5% ABV
> > Must be made from a neutral grain spirit.
>
> Our campaign was aimed at raising awareness in the drinks community and with general consumers, to question if what they are being sold is gin, or just a flavoured spirit drink with some amount of juniper used in the distillation.

Discussions took place within the industry, but little agreement was reached as to how to proceed. Not feeling it was their place to lead such a campaign, Hayman's switched to talking about their gin as being a 'True English Gin' and focusing on making gin by the existing rules.

Numerous attempts have been made to create the world's strongest gin. Swedish company Ultra Uncut developed an 82.5% ABV gin in 2018 by tweaking the production process so as to increase the intensity of the alcohol level. Two years later, Kent-based Anno Distillers created Anno Extreme 95, which 'packs more punch and flavour, drop for drop, than any other spirit in the world'. A 5ml measure results in a full-flavoured G&T with 75 per cent less alcohol than a normal 50ml measure of 40% ABV. The sheer strength of the gin is achieved by extending the distillation process and combining steeping, vapour infusion, rectification and gentle heat to result in a gin offering long, dry, complex notes with hints of warm liquorice.

Andy Reason, director of Anno Distillers said:

> It is not our intention to encourage people to drink the spirit in excess, but as with any alcohol some will no doubt do so. Our recommended servings are with 5ml of Extreme 95 plus tonic to give a full-flavoured gin with only around 25% of the alcohol of a standard double, or using 25ml Extreme 95 with tonic for a slightly stronger G&T than usual but with way more flavour. Clearly consumers can use these measures as a guide and add anywhere between to get the flavour level they prefer. We have marketed Extreme 95 in a 200cl bottle and included a measuring beaker to assist in quantity control and clearly marked the product with a high ABV warning.

Does gin cause personality changes?

Does gin encourage aggression or does it reflect personal characteristics? A study carried out by a group of psychologists at the University of Innsbruck in 2018, raised some intriguing questions. The psychologists surveyed a group of 953 people to investigate correlations between food and drink preferences and personality. The participants were given a long list of products and asked to scale them 1–6 in order of preference. They were then given a personality questionnaire designed to evaluate emotional stability, which included sections relating to Machiavellianism, aggression and a tendency towards everyday sadism. Among the questions, participants were asked if they enjoyed tormenting people. When the responses were studied, it was noted that people who enjoyed bitter food and drink tended to have more malevolent traits. Gin drinkers scored highest on these traits. The authors could find no reason for this, beyond suggesting that bitter-tasting foods could be 'compared to a roller-coaster ride where people enjoy things that induce fear'.

Chapter 10

Inspirations for Gin

A drink with its origins in vapour has inevitably become the stuff of legends and myths, whether based in reality or fiction. Elements of its history and appeal have become legends in themselves, whether true or not, such as the persistent suggestions that genever was first distilled by Sylvius de Bouve at the University of Leiden.

One of the most familiar phrases linked to gin is 'Dutch courage' reflecting the way in which gin acted as a boost to confidence. The phrase originates from a Dutch saying 'A sailor's best working compass is a glass completely full of genever.' It is probable that the English navy first encountered genever during the 1570 Battle of Antwerp, during which the English forces helped the Dutch in battles against Spain. Drinking a glass of genever became a custom of Dutch sailors and soldiers before going into battle to help steel themselves for the forthcoming fights. Similar influences would have occurred during the Thirty Years War in the seventeenth century.

Edmund Waller, poet and politician wrote

'The Dutch their Wine and all their Brandee lose,
Disarmed from that, of which their Courage grows.'

Another myth takes the opposite view, since many believe that gin can make you cry. This belief dates back to the days of the Gin Craze and William Hogarth's emotional *Gin Lane* image. There is, in fact, little truth in this myth. There is no innate quality or ingredient in gin to make people more susceptible to sadness and tears. Just like any other alcohol, gin can affect people in different ways, particularly depending on their mood. Someone who is already feeling despondent and has a glass of gin may well find themselves becoming even sadder, but the same could be true if they had chosen to drink wine, beer or vodka. Likewise, any feelings of aggression, restlessness, confidence or even feeling 'sexy' are affected by a much wider range of factors than just one type of drink. Gin has also been suggested as causing nightmares, which can happen if people drink too much alcohol before bedtime. Research has proved that alcohol does lessen sleep quality, interrupting the sleep cycle at the stage where sleepers are most likely to have vivid dreams or nightmares. Consequently, when drinking too much gin before bedtime, nightmare dreams can occur.

As mentioned previously, bathtub gin has become a very popular style. The name has caught on worldwide, with increasing numbers of gins using the name, such as Norfolk Gin's Bathtub Gin, which was initially developed in the kitchen, before being transferred to the garage where it continues to be made.

The term has even appeared in films. The 1982 film *Annie*, contains a scene in which Miss Hannigan is shown doctoring bathtub gin, while the *Simpsons* 1997 episode: 'Homer versus the Eighteenth Amendment' portrays Homer and Bart Simpson mixing and brewing gin in a bathtub within the basement. The resultant brew is then secretly distributed to Moe's Tavern. In 2018, the film *Mary Poppins Returns* starring Emily Blunt includes a scene where Mary Poppins and the Banks children swim in a magical bathtub. Mary Poppins sings a song entitled 'Can You Imagine That?' which includes the lyrics:

> Some people like to dive right in
> Can you imagine that?
> And flap about in bathtub gin
> Can you imagine that?
> Doggies paddling twenty leagues below
> Might seem real, but we know it's not so.

Many gin cocktails owe their existence to bathtub gin, as they were devised to hide the unpleasant taste of the gin itself. These include the Last Word cocktail: gin, green Chartreuse, lime juice and maraschino, and the previously mentioned Bees Knees and Gin Rickey.

Pimm's has become one of the most iconic of brands, associated with summertime and social events like Wimbledon, the Chelsea Flower Show, Ascot and Henley Royal Regatta. Many people would not even realise that it is a gin-based drink, and it is a far cry from its Victorian origins as a health tonic. The story starts in 1823, when a man named James Pimm invented and marketed a drink known as Pimm's to the customers of his oyster bar in the City of London. This was a period when people were interested in drinking 'healthy tonics', alongside breathing the sea air or taking a dip in the sea. Mr Pimm's tonic was a combination of gin combined with herbs aiding digestion. He offered the tonic in a small tankard type cup, known as the 'No 1 cup'. The drink became extremely popular, and from 1859 was sold commercially. Eventually, Mr Pimm sold the brand and the product to a Mr Frederick Sawyer, who eventually sold it to Horatio Davies, a future Lord Mayor of London. Pimm's became a drink sold throughout the British Empire. By 1887, there was even a chain of Pimm's Oyster Houses, enabling customers to drink Pimm's while enjoying a plate of oysters. The brand has maintained its position throughout all the changes of the twentieth century, creating a popular catch phrase known as 'Pimm's o'clock' as a result of one of its advertising campaigns.

Asking for a Dog's Nose would have been commonplace in the nineteenth century. It is said to have been a favourite drink of Charles Dickens and was even featured in *The Pickwick Papers*. Sam Weller was attending the Brick Lane Branch of the United Grand Junction Ebenezer Temperance Association during which the names of new converts to the Temperance Movement were announced. This included H. Walker, a tailor with a wife and two children who reports that twice a week, for twenty years, drank 'Dog's nose, which your committee find upon enquiry, to be compounded of warm porter, moist sugar, gin, and nutmeg (a groan, and "So it is!" from an elderly female).'

A similar popular drink, known as purl, is mentioned in Charles Dickens' *Our Mutual Friend*. The Six Jolly Porters is described as being well known for its purl (porter mixed with gin and served warm with various flavourings such as sugar and nutmeg), as well as dog's nose. Purl is also mentioned in *The Old Curiosity Shop*, where Dick Swiveller brews the drink.

A modern legend that is becoming increasingly promulgated is the suggestion that gin was the first item used for product placement in films, thus encouraging people to buy a particular brand. Product placement has become very sought after by brands, as it can attract a lot of attention from potential drinkers. A gin brand was definitely present in the 1951 film, *The African Queen*. There is a scene where the two stars, Katherine Hepburn and Humphrey Bogart, are trapped on a boat. Hepburn loses her patience with the drunken Bogart and tips his bottle of Gordon's Gin overboard. This has been suggested as being the first time a named product was seen clearly in a movie, but film buffs disagree, pointing to the fact that brands can be observed in movies like the Marx Brothers' films as early as the 1930s.

Gin has been associated with many famous people, including Noel Coward and Sir Winston Churchill, creating numerous modern legends. Sir Francis Chichester was the first man to sail around the world solo, leaving Bucklers Hard on the Solent on 12 August 1966. He followed the route taken by Clipper ships in years gone by. This involved a 14,000 mile route around Africa and across the Indian Ocean to Sydney Australia, before returning via the Pacific and Cape Horn – a journey taking 1517 miles. The total journey lasted 226 days.

When organising supplies for the trip, his stores list included six bottles of gin, plus twenty-four bottles of assorted spirits. He credited his success to a daily glass of Pink Gin and is reported as saying that his worst day was when the gin supply ran out. His boat, *The Gypsy Moth*, was initially preserved alongside the *Cutty Sark* in Greenwich, but when restoration was required in 2004, it was sold for £1 and a gin and tonic to the UK Sailing Academy, Cowes. After restoration, the vessel took part in a second circumnavigation of the world, as part of the Blue Water Round the World Rally. It has since been moored on the Beaulieu River, at Bucklers Hard, Hampshire.

Writer T. S. Eliot claimed that gin was one of his main sources of inspiration. In the *Letters of T. S. Eliot,* he explains how he came to write the monologue in *Sweeney Agonistes* saying, 'I wrote it in three-quarters of an hour after church time, and before lunch one Sunday morning, with the assistance of half a bottle of Booth's Gin.'

It is also reported that following a lecture at a small town near Boston, he was asked how he kept his youthful appearance. His reply became legendary 'Gin and drugs, Madam – gin and drugs!'

War-inspired gins

War is another theme that has provided inspiration for gins. D-Day Gin was created to honour the distiller's grandfather, who served as a British soldier during the Second World War, and features botanicals from the regions in which he fought. Crossing the Atlantic, Bluecoat Gin is named for the blue uniforms worn by militiamen during the War of Independence, and inspired by Philadelphia's history of innovation.

A chance meeting at an International Police Association conference between a policeman from Wearside and his equivalent from Germany led to one of the strangest gin stories. That meeting highlighted a bizarre family connection spanning three centuries, tying mining communities in both countries and resulted in the creation of a new gin importing business. Peter Meinken is a police officer whose family own a distillery in Wanne-Eickel, in the Ruhr Valley. The Eicker and Callen Distillery dates back to 1749 and produces handcrafted, triple-distilled brews. At the time of the meeting, Bryn Jones was a member of the Northumbria Police. German policeman Peter Meinken was a member of Newcastle United Football Club and regarded the North East as his second home. Peter asked Bryn for help to distribute gin made in his family's Ruhr distillery to bars and other customers within north-east England. Both the Ruhr and Bryn's hometown of Sunderland possess a coal mining heritage, and Bryn himself comes from a family of coal miners. Now retired from his work in the police force, Bryn set up the House of Ruhr in Houghton-le-Spring to import the liquors and create special brands. 'We have "Bergmann" Gin which is the German word for miner and contains Goji Berry, Physalis and Yerba Leaf amongst its botanicals while "Vogel", the German word for bird, represents the yellow canaries that saved so many miner's lives from coal gas and this has a more lemon-flavoured base,' says Bryn.

The third gin, 'Renton', is named after Bryn's maternal, great-great-grandfather Captain James Ogilvie Renton, lost at sea in 1871 and whose body was never found. It is a gin, which led to an unexpected discovery. An Irish customer, David Renton, contacted Bryn to order a bottle of Renton for his father's eightieth birthday. His father was the third generation to be called James Ogilvie Renton. Further enquiries resulted in the discovery that the two families were related, making David Bryn's fourth cousin. 'I couldn't believe that a bottle of gin could connect families together – it's sometimes called "mother's ruin" but in this case, it's more like "families united",' said Bryn.

Other bizarre connections between the various families have since appeared. Peter Meinken's grandfather worked as an army medic during the Second World War, but continued to devise gin recipes mainly for medicinal purposes. The twenty-five medics in his platoon made a promise that they would return to Meinken's drugstore for a toast at the end of the war. Although only nine of the squad remained in 1945, they kept their promise and a recipe was made to honour those men. Many of the distilleries had been damaged by the retreating German army at the end of the war, resulting in members of the Allied Forces being placed in command to rebuild the area's infrastructure and mines. Captain Jim Renton was given the task in the Ruhr, resulting in the decision to name a gin after his great-grandfather.

Geography and gin

The UK has plenty of places with a dark history lending themselves to the naming of gin brands. Tower Hill Gin is named after one of the most deadly of locations, a place where so many Tower of London prisoners were executed. During the eighteenth-century Gin Craze, there was a gin shop in every street within the City of London. The opening of the City of London Distillery in 2012 led to the creation of Authentic Gin, Square Mile Gin and Six Bells Lemon Gin. Since the distillery is within sight of St Paul's Cathedral, developing a Christopher Wren Gin was a natural choice given his involvement in the cathedral's creation.

Soho is one of the most iconic areas of London, with historical links to pornography, sleazy bars, prostitutes, as well as theatre, art and drama. The British horror comedy *Shaun of the Dead* was written in Soho, while market trader Raye du Val was a drug addict, dealer and well known to the police. The King of Soho Gin brand typifies these contrasting images. A high quality gin brand, it celebrates the life of the original 'King of Soho', Paul Raymond, who was famous for his risqué shows such as *Yes, We have no Pyjamas* strip clubs and pornography including magazines *Men Only*, *Escort* and *Mayfair*.

The King of Hearts Gin sets out to reflect Paul Raymond's life and the bohemian, hedonistic nature of the area. Bright blue or pink bottles bear the image of an elegant, top-hatted character with a hidden face. This design was carefully created to combine all the characteristics that make Soho such a vibrant and hedonistic area. A fox tail waves magnificently across the bottom of the image, signifying Soho's original status as a royal hunting ground – as well as the fox's reputation as a mischievous nocturnal creature, just like the enigmatic urban Soho. The character tips his hat as he looks at a book, reflecting the role of the creative industries in the area. Velvet tailoring highlights bohemian fashions, while the trumpet links directly to the music business.

The stormy coast of the West Country, with its heritage of wreckers, provided the inspiration for Wrecking Coast Gin, based at Tintagel in Cornwall. Black and white drawings highlight the stormy seas on every bottle.

Badachro Distillery in Scotland has adopted a similar approach, naming its highest strength gin, Storm Gin, after the storms that are experienced in the Highlands.

Death's Door Gin involves one of the most deadly of all locations: a body of water between Door County peninsula and Washington Island, in America. Legends surrounding Death's Door portray dramatic scenes of countless shipwrecks, of a huge Native American war party being pummelled to death against its rocky shores, of ships pulverised by swirling currents. Even the exact origins of the name are shrouded in legend. One story links to the destruction of the Native American war party, others refer to stories by early French and American travellers caught in storms. How much is truth and how much has been elaborated over the years is difficult to say. What is certain is that the area is well known for its destructive quality, that numerous ships have been destroyed by the violent storms that can arise in the area, with 1906 sailing directions commenting: 'There is a strong current ... and many vessels have been lost ... sailing vessels cannot make headway against it. The coast is rock-bound and certain destruction awaits the craft going ashore'. A French document from 1728 refers to the passage as Cap A La Mort, while other charts have described as Porte des Morts. The Death's Door distillers maintain the links by using juniper sourced from the area.

Rivalry between Liverpool and the Wirral is reflected in Tappers Darkside Gin. The name refers to the darkside line depicting how Liverpudlians view the Wirral, home of the gin's distillery.

In Australia, Applewoods Gin created a limited range based on the seven deadly sins – sloth, envy, lust, pride, wrath, greed and gluttony – incorporating botanicals which reflect these traits. Typical ingredients include chilli in the Gin of Wrath, green herbs wormwood and strawberry gum leaf in Envy, plus some malt spirit to spice it up, and a raspberry rich version for Lust.

Bertha's Revenge is the unusual name given to a gin from Northern Ireland. An Irish Milk Gin, it utilises whey alcohol sourced from dairy farmers in Cork, together with natural well water and a mix of locally foraged and grown botanicals. The founders of Ballyvolane House Spirits say that the gin took ten months to create from conception to birth, similar to the gestation period for a cow. At the same time, it was felt that the name Bertha's Revenge was apt since Big Bertha was a local cow with a very distinctive reputation. Reared locally, Big Bertha was a Droimeann cow from Sneem in County Kerry. She died in 1993, just three months before her forty-ninth birthday. Big Bertha had been a local celebrity, having given birth to thirty-nine calves over her lifetime. This fact, together with her age, had earned her an entry into *The Guinness Book of Records*. Her wake was held in the Blackwater Tavern, Sneem.

Croc Rock Gin combines elements of both geography and danger in its brand image. Distilled by the Isle of Cumbrae gin company, it is based on a local landmark. A rocky outcrop stretching into the sea close to Millport harbour, it first attracted attention over 100 years ago when a local man left the pub having had a few drinks. He looked at the rock and thought that it resembled a crocodile. He then set to work with a brush and paint highlighting features like a snout, teeth, eyes and scales. It quickly became a famous landmark, popular with generations of visitors keen to have their photograph taken with the crocodile. Tide times can mean that sometimes it is surrounded by the sea, thus adding to the sense of danger. As a result, Croc Rock Gin was designed to symbolise the local people's love of the crocodile, while recognising the potential danger of its bite by combining botanicals like Cacao, stem ginger and orange.

Unusual ingredients

The launch of Moonshot Gin in April 2017 by That Boutique-y Gin company made many people believe it was an April Fool's Day joke, but this could not be further from the truth. The company set out to make an extremely unusual gin by sending all the botanicals used in its distillation into near space – over 24km above the earth thus enabling them to be exposed to air pressure of less than a hundredth of normal air pressure at sea level. As the company point out, fluids in the body vaporise at just over 18km into space. The chosen botanicals – juniper, coriander, camomile flowers, fresh lemon peel, cardamom, dried bitter orange peel, cinnamon, cubeb pepper, liquorice root and angelica – were then vacuum distilled at room pressure (nearer one-tenth of that at sea level) for freshness and elegance.

That same year saw the London-based Portobello Road Gin develop the world's first pechuga gin, distilled with turkey breasts. It utilised a distilling process common to the Mexican mezcal production method. During celebratory occasions, a distiller's family would gather fruits, grains and spices before redistilling mezcal with the ingredients, thus creating a Pechuga Mezcal. The name pechuga refers to the way in which the breast of a chicken or turkey is suspended in the still and is slowly cooked by the mezcal vapours during distillation. To make their version, Portobello Road Gin was redistilled amid a group of family and friends with a mix of apples, pears, plums, currants, raisins, sultanas, apricots, brown rice, passion fruit and spices, plus a turkey breast.

During the distillation process, a small portion of gin is always lost through evaporation. This portion is known as the 'angels share' and accounts for just 1 per cent of the distillation. Cambridge

Distillery set out to capture that share, involving a special distillation process using air pressure less than half of that found on top of Mount Everest, and at temperatures lower than the South Pole so as to prevent evaporation. Only 15ml of liquid is captured at each distillation and fifty distillation cycles are needed in order to produce a tiny bottle. Branded as Watenshi, it contains unusual botanicals such as yuzu peel, shiso leaf and sesame seeds. Only six bottles were made per batch, and it was sold in hand-blown decanters at prices around £2,000 a bottle. Even more costly was London-based Jam Jar's Morus LXIV gin, made from the distilled leaves of just one ancient mulberry tree along with complementary botanicals. It was sold in handmade porcelain jars with a price tag of £4,000 each, making it one of the most expensive gins ever produced. The gin was exclusive to the Harvey Nichols department store in London.

Duncan Gilroy from Hussingtree Gin says, 'People are asking for unusual things. They are attracted by the possibility of something different.' When a local asparagus farmer asked why there were no asparagus gins, they were immediately inspired to try. Duncan Gilroy said:

> We played for five to six months with ways of using asparagus as a botanical. Eventually we dehydrated asparagus so that it became more straw/grass like, and used that as a botanical. We added some Droitwich salts in the distillation process. We thought it would a short-term thing, but it attracted a lot of attention and it was very popular. We introduced it at the Worcester Gin Festival and virtually everyone who came through the door tried it.

Tonka beans were another unusual product used. Duncan says:

> We were sitting in a hotel near Evesham talking to a chef about gin and food. He brought out this pot of tonka beans

used by chefs for flavouring. The beans have a caramel, almond, vanilla aroma and we were intrigued. We spent two months experimenting with them and blended them with one of our dry gins. We found the resultant gin went well with lemonade or cola, but not with a quinine-based tonic. It needed a mixer that was slighter sweeter than usual and caused a lot of interest.

Sandringham Gin incorporates not just ingredients from Sandringham gardens but its special sharon fruit, grown on a sheltered wall at the end of what was once a range of glasshouses paid for by the winnings of Edward VII's famous racehorse, Persimmon.

Even stranger versions of gin can be found in Australia, where you can drink gins made from ants. Inspired by Australian flora and fauna, Angry Ant Gin, made by the Bass & Flinders Distillery in Mornington, includes botanicals handpicked from the Wooleen Station, Western Australia. These include mulla mulla, purple vetch flowers, native lemongrass, sandalwood nuts, currant bush and Australian ants. Colonies of ants use pheromones to communicate, conveying messages including danger. The resultant gin uses pheromones released by the ants during distillation to create a unique gin.

Australian gin has also been made using a different type of ants: green ants, which are described as being very large, and very grumpy. Sacha La Forgia of Adelaide Hills Distillery was working with a local Aboriginal group exploring opportunities presented by native Australian plants. She was given some green ants and told to see what she could do with them. Initially very squeamish, she experimented with vapour infusion of the ants before brewing the resultant liquid extremely slowly to preserve the flavour. Leaving a few ants in the bottle to give the final touch, she tasted the liquid and discovered it was 'limey, coriander with herbaceous notes. I knew it was the perfect gin botanical.'

This Australian initiative has resulted in a similar version being developed in Europe. The Cambridge Distillery collaborated with the

Nordic Food Lab to develop Anty Gin, which contains the essence of sixty-two red wood ants giving a citrus taste, together with hand-foraged botanicals such as juniper, wild wood avens and nettle. Each bottle of Anty Gin also contains a 5cl dropper bottle of pure ant distillate, enabling drinkers to taste the pure flavour or intensify the flavour. William Lowe from the Cambridge Distillery commented:

> The reason people use ants is that they have a very specific flavour, which is best described as a very citrus flavour. We did a lot of research and found that the reason ants taste like citrus is because they spray formic acid as a method of defence. Hundreds of years ago, formic acid was made by distilling ants, and so that's what we decided to do.

Using ants in gin is designed to encourage awareness of insects as a potential food source.

A cork-infused gin was developed in Portugal. The Ginout is a venture between a distiller at the Caprioius Distillery and a cake designer. The gin is distilled with botanicals including fig leaves, olive oil and peony flowers before being matured in ex-Port casks and then macerated with toasted cork. This is said to be the first time that cork has been used as a botanical to age the spirits.

Possibly one of the most unusual gin ingredients of all was used by the Piston Distillery to produce a bespoke gin for the Morgan Motor Company. The resultant gin is infused with ash wood shavings from the wood used to make the body supporting framework of each Morgan car.

One of the stranger reactions to the 2020 Covid-19 pandemic was the growth of a consumer desire for nostalgia, especially as the end of the year dawned. With the pandemic creating a 'new normal' lifestyle, increased job insecurity, social distancing and contact with loved ones harder to achieve, familiar, comforting, nostalgic tastes were much in demand. Elements of the trend had been present for some time, but the events of 2020 proved to be the tipping point. Britain became a nation of bakers, keen to create delicious home-made cakes and biscuits. Old-fashioned sweets like sherbert lemons and pear drops were being sought out, along with familiar, reassuring brands. Yet what made this particularly unusual was the way it was not simply a return to past tastes, but a reworking of the styles, giving nostalgic products a slightly different edge. Warwickshire-based entrepreneur, Hollies Lollies, started creating large sweet sloe gin lollipops. Zmurgorium's Turkish delight gin liqueur and its Choc-o-bloc Gin instantly appealed to people seeking comforting tastes, as did salted caramel from Riverside Spirits, and Parma Violet Gin produced by numerous companies, including Whitley Neill, Wirral Distillery and Two Birds Distillery.

For many people, Blackpool is synonymous with childhood holidays or visits to the Blackpool illuminations. And what would a trip to the seaside be without a stick of rock? Not surprisingly, local entrepreneurs developed a classic pink Blackpool Rock Gin, inspired by the seaside and infused with real Blackpool gin. Across the Pennines, in northeast England, the focus is on evoking childhood ice cream memories with Lemon Top Gin – a traditional desert of vanilla ice cream topped with a dollop of lemon sorbet. As director Aaron Stoutt explained, 'there's nothing more exciting and reinvigorating than the sounds, smells and tastes of the British coast. We decided that to be authentic, our drink had to capture the essence of our favourite ice cream.'

Gins and liqueurs incorporating favourite cake and confectionary tastes attracted attention, with flavours such as Lemon Drizzle Cake and Bakewell Tart. Zmurgorium went further by turning to an even earlier dessert, syllabub, setting out to recreate the flavour with a frothy mix of lemon, lime and warm oats.

One gin company that specifically set out to capitalise on this trend for traditional cakes was the North Yorkshire-based Mrs Cuthbert's. Taking its name from the founder's Aunty Dot, better known as Mrs Dorothy Cuthbert, Aunty Dot had been a keen home baker during the 1940s – delighting friends and family with sweet delights such as Bakewell tart, muffins, Victoria sponge, and rhubarb and custard crumble.

Dunnet Bay Distillers launched a special Clootie Dumpling Gin inspired by a traditional Scottish pudding wrapped in a cloth (cloot) as it cooked – clearly illustrated with a nostalgic black and white label bearing the image of a cook busy in the kitchen. The resultant gin combines notes of juniper with raisins, treacle, nutmeg and allspice.

Gravity Drinks turned to confectionery for nostalgic inspiration, creating a range of sherbet gin liqueurs in retro lemon, raspberry and orange flavours evoking a 1960s ambiance 'taking you back to when love was free, hair was big and revolution was in the air'. The resultant gins possessed a punchy real sherbet kick complete with an added glitter shimmer effect, while the bottles incorporated a retro design.

One of the most iconic of all biscuits is the Jaffa Cake, an irresistible mix of chocolate, orange and sponge. Opinions differ as to whether they are cakes or biscuits, but they are definitely a timeless, irresistible treat. Jaffa Cake Gin set out to capture that magic, the links between past and present, with teatimes and snack times across the years. Distilled with oranges, fresh orange peel, cocoa powder and Jaffa Cakes, the resultant gin became so popular that it had its own website.

Chapter 11

Fantastical Gins

When it comes to developing a brand, distillers often focus on the darker side of gin, whether it is redolent of Hogarth's memorable Gin Lane images, stories that appeal to the darker side of the human psyche, ghosts and demons or simply dark geographical locations.

Ghostly gins

Images of skulls dominate the website for Edinburgh's Old Poison Distillery. Every label contains a skull, while one even includes an image of a snake curled around a bottle full of a black liquid, with venom dripping from a grinning skull. The founders decided to use the Old Poison name due to the ancient medicinal uses of juniper, which may or may not have always been successful. Distillers in Iceland opted for an equally dark image, that of the Black Death, creating a gin which is now produced in Warrington. The top-hatted skull with its sly grin decorating the label never fails to attract attention.

Known as one of Europe's most haunted cities, York has hundreds of ghosts haunting the city's pubs, streets, hotels and theatres. One of those ghosts is now featured on gin bottles belonging to York Gin. The Grey Lady is said to be a friendly ghost haunting the York Theatre Royal. In her honour, York Gin created a Grey Lady Gin, distilled with Earl Grey tea and infused with pea flower to create a hauntingly spectral blue-grey hue. Customers are told about the ghost whenever they buy Grey Lady Gin from the York Gin Shop, as apparently the staff 'love nothing better than telling a good ghost story'. York Gin is adjacent to the Golden Fleece pub, where ghost-hunters often stay overnight in the haunted bedroom in hope of meeting some of the ghosts on the premises.

Visitors to the premises of Plymouth Gin often experience unusual sightings and feelings of ghostly presences. This is the oldest working gin distillery in England, and occupies a building dating back to the early 1300s. Known as Black Friars, it was even a debtors' prison at one point. Several paranormal investigators have sought to unearth the truth behind its ghostly mysteries. There are reports of a young girl who meanders around the corridors, while a man named Charles haunts the still room. Women often report a feeling of dread, and move quickly away from the ladies rest room. A medium working with Haunted Devon reported:

> A World War II lady was stabbed here. The gasp sensation reflects where the knife penetrated her. Her death was the result of an argument over personal belongings in the shelter. Her assailant was another woman who was in uniform and wearing long green socks. ... The whole issue was covered up and forgotten given the circumstances of the time (1941 during the Blitz). The victim had few/no relatives so she was easy to dispose of. There were threats to keep quiet about it or access would be denied to the shelter.

The medium also indicated that just inside the entrance to the Distillery 'someone was hung in this area and the corpse was left to rot.' Elsewhere in the building, the medium commented: 'There is a lower area underground – or lower than it is today. This was used to hold people but much of this was not legally binding. People were put in here if they owed money or rent. The conditions were terrible and the area was divided up, possibly into cells.'

In Scotland, the Glenrothes Whisky Distillery is said to be haunted by a gin-loving ghost. Biawa 'Byeway' Makalunga was originally born in Zimbabwe during a period of famine. Major Grant, owner of the distillery, was on a hunting expedition in the area and decided to take Biawa back to Scotland as his servant, initially as a pageboy, and later as a footman and general servant. When Major Grant died in 1931, provision was made for his heirs to maintain Biawa who eventually spent the rest of his life living in an apartment at Clan Grant House, and was buried in a grave overlooking the distillery. When a new still house was opened in 1980, there were reports that Biawa had been sighted throughout the distillery. His spirit is still remembered in the form of 'a toast to the ghost' before each tasting of a new batch of whisky. However, it is certain that Biawa would not have been searching for a dram of whisky as he disliked it, preferring gin and tonic.

For gin enthusiasts seeking ghostly encounters, the Viaduct Tavern near St Paul's has become a popular venue. Built in 1869, the building is a late Victorian gin palace. It was built on the site of Old Newgate Gaol, where hundreds of executions and hangings took place. Thousands more people were imprisoned here, and the debtors' cells remain in existence, albeit transformed into the tavern cellars. On the ground floor is an unusual token booth located behind the bar. Distrusting her staff, a former landlady installed the booth. People had to buy tokens direct from her in the booth, before ordering their gin. The upper floor of the pub is rumoured to have been an opium den and has a very spooky atmosphere. Many of the pub staff are said to be reluctant to climb the stairs for fear of seeing a mystery woman in white. Poltergeists have been heard at work in the cellar, while the sounds of loud bangs and footsteps have been heard from upstairs. Staff have reported instances of being touched by invisible hands.

For centuries, surgeons and barbers worked side by side. Barber surgeons were responsible for everything from cutting hair to pulling teeth and amputating limbs, including letting blood – a popular way of treating illness. In 1745, at the height of the Gin Craze, George II ordered that the two professions should be permanently separated. As a result, barbers become solely responsible for shaving, cutting and styling hair. Their shops were popular venues, where men gathered ro chat while waiting their turn in the barber's chair. Providing drinks for sale was the obvious money-making option for enterprising barbers. Gin was the drink of choice, cheap and easily available from hundreds of distillers – or even home distilled on the premises, especially since alcohol was needed as a lotion for shaving purposes. As the years progressed, gin became an essential ingredient for barbers. Barbers Gin reflects that history, and like the gins of the eighteenth century, it does not contain any citrus botanicals, just juniper, coriander, thyme and angelica root.

The use of botanicals and herbs in gin distilling provide a link with witchcraft – and the potential for creating some witchy gins has not been missed. The Dorset Drinks Company has a Witchcraft Gin utilising a variety of botanicals including a tropical plant known as *Clittoria ternata* reputed to have various qualities including anti-stress, enhancing, tranquilising and sedative properties. An extra magical quality is given by the fact that when tonic is added to the gin, the colour changes before the drinker's eyes.

In Wales there is the tale of the Welsh Witch, referring to the folklore of North Wales as she uses a magical cauldron to concoct potions giving wisdom and inspiration:

> From the Welsh haunted hills comes a tale of a Witch,
> Lives by the sun and loves by the moon
> She possesses a potion of which?
> Distilled to perfection and infused botanically
> By this beautiful enchantress so magically,
> Cleansed and inspired with love and light
> This mysterious Welsh Witch of the night.

Legends of a curse set amid the shadows of Pendle Hill, Lancashire, led to the creation of Peddlers Pins Gin, based on a local legend. It was 18 March 1612 when Alison Device, granddaughter of Demdike, a notorious local witch, was on her way to Trawden Forest. She passed a peddler from Halifax, named John Law, and asked him for a pin. Metal pins were expensive as they were handmade, but were essential ingredients for magical purposes. The peddler refused and walked away. According to reports, Alison's 'familiar spirit' appeared in the shape of a dog and asked if she would harm John Law. She ordered the dog to lame the peddler. Instantly, John Law fell to the ground, paralysed down one side and unable to speak. He was taken to a local inn to recover, where Alison came and begged his forgiveness, as she was sorry for what she had done. He forgave her, but his son Abraham was less content. Abraham complained to the local magistrate, leading to a number of arrests. By the end of April, nineteen people had been imprisoned in Lancaster Castle for suspected witchcraft and were eventually put to death. Inspired by the stories of witchcraft, the distiller began to research the botanicals used by the seventeenth-century Pendle Witches. The resultant gin contains a selection of botanicals with a list of their potential properties:

Angelica to ward off evil, bring good fortune and a harmonious home life
Apple the fruit of the gods
Cherry the fruit of immortality
Cinnamon for abundance, protection and love
Coriander for good health
Hibiscus used in love spells as it is a potent aphrodisiac
Jasmine for healthy dreams and meditation
Juniper provides good luck in love and attraction
Lavender ensures peace and purification
Lemon calming and healing
Mint when grown in the garden brings good luck
Rosemary to enhance intuition and psychic abilities
Sage cleansing and healing
Thyme for good health, attracts fortune and courage.

Yet there is only one gin that has the honour of being cursed by a professional witch. This is the Evil Spirit Gin, produced in the English village of Pluckley. According to the *Guinness Book of World Records*, Pluckley is England's most haunted village, possessing at least twelve ghosts including Screaming Woods, a phantom Monk, and Lady Dering (also known as the Red Lady), who died in the twelfth century. Even the ingredients of the bright green Evil Spirit Gin have a taste of the occult as it includes mint, apples and a dash of Devil's Claw. Union distillers sought the help of a professional witch, Ms Julianne White, who 'cursed' it by casting bespoke enchantments under a full moon in October. Apparently the enchantments 'empower the drinker to follow whatever their hearts desire – whether it is for good or evil', but the distributors Moonpig do make one recommendation. Don't drink it under a full moon since 'Moonpig is not responsible if you're transformed into a toad, zombie, or werewolf.'

Gin and horror

The inherent dark images of gin have invariably formed a link with images of horror, such as vampires, Halloween and dark feasts. The pretty Yorkshire coastal town of Whitby is dominated by the eerie abbey ruins standing high above the harbour. According to the writer, Bram Stoker, Dracula's ship was wrecked just off the coast and he came ashore in the shape of giant black dog, making his first kill in the graveyard below the abbey. Not surprisingly, Whitby has become a focus for Goth-style activities, and Whitby Gin has taken these dark stories for its inspiration. Jess Slater of Whitby Gin says:

> Having Whitby Abbey on our doorstep means we have the perfect starting point. We get our inspiration from the grounds, and the many stories which have inspired the place such as Bram Stoker, Whitby Witches and the Shadowmancer to name but a few. Once we have a name we

set about developing a recipe which is authentic to the source. A good example is our Demeter edition, which is named after Dracula's ship, the *Demeter*, and is made using local botanicals such as the heather from the moors Stoker would have known. Plums were chosen due to the fact that they are a favourite food among bats, one of the animals into which Dracula could transform.

Other Goth-themed gins have included Stoker and Barghest, the latter being aged in barrels shipped over from a manufacturer in the mountains of Transylvania. Working with the organisers of local events such as the town's Goth festival and the Dark Days festival are extremely important to Whitby Gin as it enables them to link their theme directly with interested consumers.

Exmoor's Wicked Wolf Distillery sums up not just the area, but also the owner's personal interests. Owner Pat Patel commented:

Wicked Wolf was the name of an old pub in Clerkenwell where my wife and I met. It closed down but I loved the name so bought it. I'm also very keen on Hammer Horror so when years later we moved to Exmoor to open a distillery, it was the ideal name linking werewolves, the wildness of Exmoor, stories of the Exmoor Beast, and the dark, tragic story of Lorna Doone. As soon as people see the logo and references to silver bullet, and the stories of the Exmoor Beast they love the branding and the concept.

Equally atmospheric is the Dead King's Gin, based around the concept of Egyptian mummies. A creation of The Boutique-y Gin Company, the aim is to focus on the aromas encountered with a freshly unwrapped Egyptian mummy. In the nineteenth century, unwrapping a mummy was a big social event with people gathering to watch each layer being removed. Consequently, the gin uses the aromatics reminiscent of embalming that would have traditionally been utilised in the embalming process such as rosemary, honey, moss and myrrh. Even the bottle sets out to highlight the Egyptian theme, being heavily etched with hieroglyphics, decorated in gold and jewels, while the lid is shown to be slightly ajar.

At first sight, the Aviation Gin brand founded by actor Ryan Reynolds seems far removed from dark associations. Based on pre-Prohibition-era American gin recipes, it is a light gin suitable for use in cocktails. Yet behind the Aviation images lie some darker links – Ryan Reynolds made his money and his name by starring in some of the darkest films ever made – *Deadpool* and *The Amityville Horror*. The latter film was based on the story of spooky encounters resulting in death and destruction when the Lutz family moved into a murder house during the 1970s.

Chef Heston Blumenthal created one of the most dramatic of all gin-linked horror feasts during his *Fantastical Feasts* TV series. His aim was to create a Gothic horror meal based on the Gothic novel. Explaining the concept, he 'took the spirit of Romanticism and added a few more astringent ingredients – a spot of violence, a dash of the supernatural, a smattering of paranoia' into his dramatic version. Romanticism was a period where picturesque scenes were prized, and Gothic tastes added mysterious faces at doors and shadowy figures to create a sense of horror. Blumenthal was focusing on the period when Bram Stoker's *Dracula* and Robert Louis Stevenson's *Dr Jekyll and Mr Hyde* had been published. Much of his inspiration for the gin-based drink was taken from the story of *Dr Jekyll and Mr Hyde* due to the dramatic personal transformation that takes place. The compound used by Jekyll (described as white powder to which a red tincture is added 'brightens in colour, to effervesce audibly, and to throw off small fumes of vapour … before changing to a dark purple, then fading again more slowly to a watery green'), inspired Blumenthal to create a very special drink for the feast. 'I needed to create a green drink that fizzed and smoked when a white powder was added to it,' he said.

Gin made the perfect choice due to its links with the eighteenth-century Gin Craze, and Hogarth's classic *Gin Lane* images containing scenes reminiscent of the horror genre such as coffins containing corpses, a child falling out of its mother's arms to death, men gnawing on bones and lots of skeletal figures.

To create his special gin drink, Heston Blumenthal utilised flavours and textures to give a fantastical, Gothic horror ambiance. Initially, he considered absinthe because of its reputation for inducing madness and stupefaction, but the colour was wrong, so the required green colour was created by a special technique using a heat-resistant setting gel, plus green food colouring. Small amounts of diced cucumber were used to provide crunch to a warm mixture of gin, tonic water and sugar. This enabled Blumenthal to create 'tiny vibrant green spheres (not unlike frogs' legs) by sucking up the liquid in a pipette and expelling it drop by drop into a beaker full of oil. The spheres burst in the mouth to create hits of flavour, intensifying the sensory experience. He then worked on the idea by putting the spheres in a Martini glass, on top of some gin granite. Dry ice was used to create a fragrant effervescence which he discovered 'spreads out wraith-like, it takes all the aroma with it'. Pellets were ground up in a pestle and mortar to create a white powder.

Guests at the feast were required to make their own gin potion. They were each presented with a cocktail comprising a set of test tubes complete with flavourings, and a flask attached to a tube. Their task was to empty the test tubes into the flask, together with a white powder plus the hot liquid containing the cucumber juice. The stopper was placed on the top of the flask and then the tube was placed into a glass filled with gin. As they watched, the dry ice vapour gradually bubbled into the glass, infusing it with the secret ingredients. Accompanying the gin potion were dishes including Dracula's Little Bites, Hestonstein's Monster (an edible skeleton complete with ingredients like deep fried brains, bone-marrow-on-the-bones, deep fried crispy eel bones) and ending with a Gourmand's Graveyard possessing edible gravestones, soil, coffins and breasts.

Outlaws

Living on the edge of society, outlaws have always possessed dark connotations and ideally fit into gin branding. Both Guy Fawkes and Dick Turpin feature in York's history, which is why York Gin was inspired to create Outlaw – winner of a Double Gold at the San Francisco World Spirits Competition in 2019. The company says:

> With York Gin Outlaw we wanted to do two things – to take inspiration from these York characters living life very close to the edge, by making a very strong gin we could imagine them drinking. But we also wanted to create a gin that was incredibly smooth – to surprise the modern drinker with the quality of our navy-strength gin. We inverted the label to make it predominantly black, which did the trick to give it that hint of menace.

By far the most well known of all outlaws is Robin Hood. Nottingham micro distillery, Redsmith, was set to create a navy-strength Outlaw Gin but hit problems when trying to trademark the name. A firm of solicitors, specialists in the intellectual property sector, contacted them on behalf of an Aberdeenshire-based company, the Outlaw Rum Company, which had trademarked the name 'outlaw' in all spirit categories, thus preventing Redsmith from marketing an outlaw gin. Wayne Asher commented: 'Outlaw seemed the perfect name as no other county in Britain has an outlaw more famous than Robin Hood.'

Fellow Nottingham distillers, Weavers, is located directly opposite Nottingham Castle and close to the Robin Hood statue, giving it added impetus to incorporate elements of the Robin Hood theme within its gin brands. Weavers Castle Gate Gin takes its inspiration from Sherwood Forest and the Robin Hood associations. Unusually, the taste is based on acorns collected during foraging expeditions in Sherwood Forest and nearby woods by distiller Mary Treese and her family. This ingredient gives the gin a very nutty taste.

Twenty-first century explosion of interest

The twenty-first century has seen an explosion of interest in myth and magic, helped by the activities of a boy wizard named Harry Potter. Countless activities and events of all kinds have been inspired by this magical interest even within the gin industry. Visitors to The Cauldron cocktail bar in Stoke Newington, London (or The Cauldron's outlets in Edinburgh and New York) are able to wave a magic wand to obtain a Unicorn Blood cocktail from a unicorn's head. The bright pink cocktail is made from a combination of freshly made syrups, juices and gin. There is no limit on the number of drinks that are provided in this way, but as The Cauldron points out, 'magic wands do not protect against hangovers'. Anyone wanting an even more magical experience can book a session in the 'potions' classroom full of bubbling brews, brooms and magical books. During the session, participants brew a range of gin-based cocktails involving a working magic wand to brew molecular cocktails that bubble, smoke and change colour.

Matthew Cortland, founder of The Cauldron says:

Our mission is to bring fantasy to life with science, technology and design and so our team of engineers and prop makers seek creative ways to make magic real for our customers. Magical

creatures from mythology are such a fun way to do that and
the unicorn, as one of the most well-known mythological
creatures is a perfect fit. If you like gin, then The Cauldron
is a good place to visit!

Legendary creatures frequently appear on gin bottles. Among the
many ethereal-based gins are Pixie Tears, Unicorn Tears, Cherubin,
Archangel, Janus, Gargoyles.

The Isle of Wight-based Mermaid Gin was inspired by its main
botanical, rock samphire, which is known locally as a 'mermaid's kiss'.
Samphire is found on the cliffs around the island, making the high
tide point on its beaches. The local legend is that like the kiss of the
mythical mermaid which saved sailors lost at sea, so the presence of
rock samphire indicated that shipwrecked sailors could feel confident
they were no longer at risk from the raging sea.

Wyverns, mythical dragon-like creatures, adorn the logo of Wessex
Gin who opted for bottles inspired by ancient potion bottles. A coin
is suspended around the neck of each bottle. These coins are an exact
replica of an Alfred the Great coin, of which the distillery possesses
one of the three remaining originals. This was the first coin to have
the monarch's face presented on it.

In Scotland, Brewdog uses mythical images to conjure up
atmosphere around its various brands. In describing its Lone Wolf
Gin, Brewdog writes 'Born under a hazy moon, Lone Wolf rose
from the ferocity of the Scots Forest. Lavender and citrus notes run
alongside a forage of feral pine needles, but it's the fierce juniper
backbone that stands this gin tall.'

Over on the Isle of Man, the Fynoderee Distillery takes its branding
from fantasy and legend. The name Fynoderee is derived from ancient
Manx folklore from the northern part of the island, where the last
Manx juniper tree was reputed to have grown – and where juniper is
now being reintroduced. The mythical, magical style carries through

to all the brand labels incorporating nature and creatures such wind spirits, the Udereek, Prince of the Elfin kind, and all manner of fairies.

In Bruges, the Black Swan Gin inherited its unusual name from a very rare event linked to the city's swans. White swans glide serenely around the canals of Bruges, and are very carefully looked after by the townsfolk as a result of a punishment imposed many centuries earlier. In 1482, Bruges fell under the control of Maximilian, the Holy Roman Emperor. He issued laws prohibiting various festivals and fairs, leading to a major revolt. Eventually the people of Bruges captured Maximilian and imprisoned him in a house called the Craenenburg. As Maximilian still would not give in, the people of Bruges executed his head squire and best friend. Eventually Maximilian gave in and revoked the law, but imposed an eternal punishment for the death of his friend. Since his friend's escutcheon contained the image of a swan, Maximilian ordered that the people of Bruges had to take care of 101 white swans for eternity. If they failed, Bruges would decay. The swans are still there today – and only white swans ever appear on the waters of Bruges. The exception was in 2014, when a black swan perched among the white swans causing a huge commotion within the city before it mysteriously disappeared. No one knows what happened to it, but the story inspired a gin named after this unique character.

Perhaps one of the most famous of all legendary creatures is the Loch Ness Monster. It is said that the first sighting of the monster took place in 565 AD, when it attacked a servant of St Columba who then forced it back into the water. Over the centuries, stories of the monster have continued, often linked to images of the legendary kelpie and water horses. From the 1930s onwards, there have been several reported sightings of the Loch Ness Monster. Many people have been convinced they have seen a huge creature amid the deep water of the loch. The story has captured the imagination of people worldwide, resulting in thousands of people visiting the area every year in hope of spotting a glimpse of this mysterious creature. A special Loch Ness Legends Gin was created by a local family, who have lived in the area for several generations. The gin is distilled on the banks of the loch and blended using a private water supply. Each small batch of gin is slightly different, with the aim of encouraging people to discover more about the magic of the region.

One company which has specialised in fantastical gin is Imaginaria, with its strapline of 'the Fantastical elixirs and tonics'. These range from the pure fantasy of legend such as Unicorn Dreams offering a taste of soft, silkiness with vanilla, marshmallow essences, to the modern fantasies such as a Pornstar Martini. Its promotional literature encourages the drinker to 'indulge your cheeky side with this delightful blend of passion fruit, vanilla and lime blended to create a taste sensation you'll remember long after the cameras stop rolling!' adding 'As the Victorians say "a glimpse of stocking can be so shocking … but a sip of this is simply bliss!"'

Chapter 12

Gin Worldwide

Wherever you go in the world, you can find gin – but it might not always be what you expect. There are some very dark and strange versions to be found, often using some extremely unusual ingredients which can arouse feelings of revulsion among some drinkers. Although certain brand names and tastes are global, others are regional or local to one country.

By far the most popular of all gins is London Dry Gin. This can be found worldwide, but has little to do with London. Although it is often assumed that London Dry Gin comes from the UK capital, the term refers to the method of distillation rather than the location. In Annex 11, Section 22, of Regulation (EC) no 110/2008 issued by the European Parliament and Council, it is officially stated that London Dry Gin is 'obtained exclusively from ethyl alcohol of agricultural origin, with a maximum methanol content of 5 grams per hectolitre of 100% vol. alcohol, whose flavour is introduced exclusively through the re-distillation in traditional stills of ethyl alcohol in the presence of all the natural plant materials used'. Once the distillation is complete, no artificial flavourings or additives can be introduced.

Only a few gins are required to be made in a specific location. These include Mahon Gin from Menorca, Vilnius Gin from Lithuania and Plymouth Gin from Plymouth UK.

The Gin Renaissance at the beginning of the twenty-first century reawakened interest in gin, especially among younger drinkers. Despite the fact that gin sales in Europe, America and Australia have rocketed since the millennium, the greatest amount of gin consumption is not found in these areas.

Asia

The largest majority of gin drinkers worldwide are located in the Philippines. Records reveal that they drink around 43 per cent of the world's gin, accounting for approximately 22 million cases annually. Much of this gin is the local brand known as Ginebra San Miguel, an 80% proof Dutch-type gin. Gin drinking is a key element in Filipino culture, and every time a bottle is opened it is customary for a shot of gin to be poured on the floor to share with the ancestral spirits. Filipinos frequently take part in evening street-based gin drinking sessions known as Ginuman. To drink gin is regarded as an attractive, joyous event, with gin brands promoted in every form of activity from newspapers to sports. The Barangay Gin Kings are one of the most popular of all Filipino basketball teams, and are sponsored by San Miguel. The team's connections with gin go back a long way, and it has previously been known as Gilbey's Gin and Gordon's Gin Boars.

The onset of the Covid-19 pandemic affected all aspects of life around the globe. Japan had been preparing to hold the 2020 Olympics in Tokyo, anticipating the arrival of 40 million tourists. Many bars and drinking establishments had ordered massive quantities of beer ready for the influx. As the pandemic took hold, and international travel came to an end, the Tokyo Olympics had to be postponed. Quite apart from the additional beer stocks, the impact of the pandemic meant that bars and restaurants saw a massive drop in customers as well as cancelled export orders. Drinkers were not going out for a drink. This resulted in gallons of beer going to waste. Kiuchi Brewery based in Naka City, Japan devised a solution – it turned surplus beer into gin. In April 2020, Kiuchi Brewery launched a 'Save Beer Spirits' campaign under which bars and brewers could turn unused beer, a product with a four- to six-month shelf life, into gin possessing a much longer expiration date. Kiuchi were able to achieve this by distilling the beer into a high proof neutral spirit, which was distilled a second time using juniper berries and botanicals to add flavour. For every 100 litres of beer sent back, Kiuchi was able to distil 8 litres of gin, or enough to fill eight 750ml bottles. Companies could choose between standard bottles, a keg or cans of sparkling gin cocktails.

Kiuchi was not the only Japanese company to take this action. The Ethical Spirits & Co was founded in February 2020 to turn left over sake kasu (the lees left over from sake production) into spirits. With the fall in beer sales due to the pandemic, it too began devising recipes to turn beer into gin. In May, Ethical Spirits was given 20,000 litres of expiring Budweiser from drinks giant AB InBev. This was used to create 4,500 bottles of gin under the Revive brand, flavoured with lemon peel, beech wood, cinnamon and san'onto, a dark, sweet sugar.

Africa

One of the effects of Imperialism and colonial activity has been the way in which the classic gin and tonic has become a staple part of African drinking habits. Once it arrived on African shores, distillers began creating African versions using local botanical flavours such as varieties of fynbos. South Africa, particularly the Western Cape, has over 9,000 unique plant species making it one of the most diverse in the world. A Mari Gin uses Atlantic Ocean water in its distillation, resulting in the creation of mineral rich, spicy, floral gins.

In Ghana, gin plays an important role in official visits. Journalist Elizabeth Ohene noted that:

> Before party politicians can enter a town or village to canvass for votes, they have to go and pay a courtesy call on the chiefs. The manufacturers of Schnapps and Gin must surely be the only ones who are producing at full capacity and maybe even doing extra shifts. An alarming amount of gin is involved in the palace ritual.

A message is sent to the chief to alert him to that an active politician is coming to see him and that requires two bottles of gin. When the active politician and his entourage arrive, they will be late getting to the palace, and they will have more bottles of gin with them.

In 2020, the Disgusting Food Museum in Malmo, Sweden held an exhibition on alcohol. Prominent among its exhibits was a Ugandan gin brand called Kasese, which is a very potent spirit made from fermented bananas. It is so powerful that unwary drinkers are advised to avoid drinking it neat. Brewed from bananas and millet, with added juniper, the result is a clear, spicy liquid, which is triple brewed to reach an alcohol content of 96%, before being blended to become 40% proof.

It is based on a traditional drink known as *enguli*, which was discovered when the British colonised Uganda in the nineteenth century. *Enguli* was regarded as a war spirit because it gave soldiers Dutch courage before battle commenced, as well as warding off flies and mosquitos. Over the years, *enguli* became so potent that by 1965 it was ordered that all production should be limited to companies with legal licences and distilled only by the East African Distillers. Although the law still exists, it is rarely enforced. Homebrew versions are common, but can be lethal. Known as 'war gin', it is often sold in jerry cans and is manufactured using sugar cane or bananas, resulting in a taste that varies from smooth to sulphuric acid flavour. It often contains methanol and in 2010, eighty people died due to methanol-contaminated Waragi causing multiple organ failure. Some communities are said to give newborn babies Waragi immediately after the birth as part of initiation rituals.

Australasia

The gin industry in Australia has expanded quickly, resulting in the creation of over 200 distilleries in less than ten years, thus reflecting changing consumer tastes, as well as alterations in Australian distillery laws. There is a preference for refreshing rather than sweet drinks, matching demands for healthy, low carbohydrate beverages. Most distillers are now focusing on the use of Australian native species to create terroir-style gins with ingredients like finger limes, myrtle and Tasmanian pepper berries.

Australia is home to the Four Pillars Gin, which has been described as being the gin versions of Willy Wonka and P.J. Barnum due to the unusual ideas the company has developed, such as a Sticky Carpet Gin. This is beer-inspired gin, based on memories of old-style pubs and bars with their sticky carpets and blaring TVs. Four Pillars Bloody Shiraz Gin evokes dark thoughts of Dracula and barber surgeons, but is actually the result of macerating Shiraz grapes in the gin.

Wildspirit, another Australian distiller, created a very different type of Bloody Gin. The company is known for its irreverent style, and so its Bloody Merry Gin contains some very unconventional infusions – celery and cherry tomatoes. Its twist on the name and label matched its unorthodox, cheeky approach as it involves a black and white cartoonish style designed to convey all aspects of the brand's story. It has been described as being 'two parts Jeeves and Wooster insanity, one part Art Nouveau, with a jigger of *Mad* magazine thrown in'. The intricate image comprises a Bacchanalian scene inspired by accounts of how new gin infusions are tested out on friends at dinner parties. It is a wild and messy inspiration process. At the centre of the picture is an elegant man dispensing gin from a bubbling copper still. All around him are people giggling, having fun, clearly intoxicated while other people are peeping from underneath the table obviously having drunk too much. There is even the odd leg or foot sticking out signalling participants who have passed out. A dog is grabbing food off the table; there are half empty containers and plates while other food is being tipped up. It is a very boisterous sampling party. The label also contains red splashes indicating where the red tomatoes have been figuratively splattered.

New Zealand has developed its own idiosyncratic gin industry, with over fifty distillers crafting gins that use native plants such as kawakawa, manuka, horopito. Gin has become one of the most popular spirits in the country resulting in events like A Celebration of Gin, and Gincredible. New Zealand gin is exported worldwide, while its highly sought-after Scrapegrace gin has been named the best dry gin in the world. Formerly trading as Rogue Society, the brand had quickly become New Zealand's top selling premium gin and was being widely exported. Success seemed guaranteed, until an American brewing company with a beer called Rogue – a brand trademarked in Asia and Canada – sent in their lawyers. The result was a trademark legal battle, which eventually resulted in Rogue Society changing its brand name in favour of Scrapegrace (an eighteenth-century word for rogue) and completely rethinking its export strategy.

Europe

Gin tourism has become big business throughout Europe. The National Jenever Museum, in Schiedam in the Netherlands and the Jenevermuseum, Hasselt, Belgium attract thousands of visitors every year, keen to discover the historical background and traditional techniques of making genever. Numerous special events are held, such as Schiedam Stokers Festival and it is possible to see how genever was made to the Old Holland method, which used huge batter trays, cooling vessels and copper stills. A recipe from 1700 is used at Schiedam to brew a traditional malt wine gin. Unusually, Schiedam even has an escape room allowing visitors to hunt for a secret recipe against a strict time limit. The giant windmills of Schiedam are an extremely picturesque aspect of the history of genever. Although there are only six of the original thirty giant Schiedam windmills surviving, visitors are able to explore the role of the millers at Walvic. Other genever attractions within the town include the Porters House, recalling the unusual way porters were employed to carry sacks of grain to the distillery. When a bell was rung, everyone rushed into the house and threw a dice. The person who threw the highest number won the job.

Countless gin distilleries across Europe offer gin making workshops, tasting events and distillery tours. In the Pennines, visitors are taken on guided walks to forage for botanicals to use in their bespoke gin. Such activities are extremely popular and gin companies are keen to take advantage of the demand. Visitor centres are frequently added when setting up new distilleries, while in Sweden the Herno Gin company plans to develop Harnosand as an international destination for gin experiences complete with a gin-themed hotel.

USA

It was the boom in American craft distilleries which helped revitalise gin in the UK. Thousands of craft brands now exist across America, and this has resulted in the creation of a specific type of gin which is now made everywhere in the world. Often described as New American or Western Gin, reflecting the region in which it started, this type of gin focuses on citrus notes rather than juniper flavour. It also tends to use a wider range of grains like corn, rye and barley to create the base spirit.

Individual American state laws can create problems for unwary distillers seeking to export gin to America as regulations can vary. In 2019, Bacardi, owner of the Bombay Sapphire brand, found itself unexpectedly at the focus of a court action together with its Florida stockists, Winn-Dixie supermarkets. A Florida resident, Uri Marrache, from Miama Dade County, purchased a bottle of the gin and drank it. He then brought a lawsuit against the companies based on Florida's Deceptive and Unfair Trade Practices Act 'individually and on behalf of all persons similarly situated' accusing the distillers of producing an 'adulterated spirit' which the Winn-Dixie chain had knowingly sold. At the heart of the issue was the fact that the distillers had used a botanical known as 'grains of paradise'. This particular botanical had been outlawed in Florida since 1868. According to Uri Marrache, 'when consumed, grains of paradise have been known for their warming and digestive properties' with the seeds being used for 'medicinal purposes' to 'treat impotence and stimulate miscarriages when a pregnancy is unwanted'. In his complaint, Marrache did not claim that he had received any physical injury as a result of ingesting the drink, nor that it had prevented any enjoyment of the drink. His lawsuit pointed out that adulterating alcohol is a 'felony of the third degree' in Florida, resulting in a potential sentence of up to five years' imprisonment, and a fine of $15,000.

Marrache went on to allege that the distillers had taken part in 'unfair methods of competition, unconscionable acts or practices and unfair or deceptive acts in the conduct of its trade or commerce'. Due to the damage this had caused to him and others, he was bringing forth a class action proposing damages for each plaintiff and indicated that there could be 'hundreds of thousands' of potential participants plus legal fees. When the case came to court in February 2020, it was dismissed on the grounds that he had not experienced any injury, and that Federal Law of 1958 covered the 'advancing food technology by permitting the use of food additives at safe levels'.

It is not just grains of paradise that can cause problems for unwary gin distiller. Doug Walford, from Afterthought Gin says:

> In the UK we use meadowsweet to make our gin different. In the US this is a poisonous plant according to the FDA, and cannot be used even though the infusion route means there is hardly any actual product in it. Liquorice root is another problem botanical as there are US restrictions on the percentage that can be used. We had to review our product for the US market and use a different botanical.

Chapter 13

What Lies Ahead?

Having recovered from coping with issues of mass alcoholism, social disfavour and being regarded as 'uncool', the revitalisation of the gin industry stumbled as it encountered unexpected problems and dark challenges to the way it operates.

Between 2010 and 2020, new gin distilleries proliferated around the world. The majority of these distilleries were artisan companies offering just a small selection of specially crafted gin brands, often linked into their immediate locality. No one knows exactly how many brands and gin distillers exist worldwide simply because the number changes so rapidly. New gins emerge almost every week. Prior to the Covid pandemic, Ginspiration, a German blog, counted 5,498 gins across 68 different countries of which 1,722 were listed for the UK. The next largest grouping was the US with 702, and Germany with 692.

Within the UK, the Wines and Spirits Trade Association only began collecting data on gin sales and gin brands in 2010 when around 50 gin brands were available. By 2013, there were 152 distilleries in the UK, most of which were in Scotland. This figure grew dramatically over the next few years, reaching 560 by early 2021. Sales of gin were equally impressive, resulting in 83 million bottles being sold in 2019, totalling over £2.6 billion. Instead of stocking just one or two gins, pubs and other licensed premises were creating gin menus complete with an extensive list of gin brands and mixers.

As demand rose, artisan distillers often encountered major issues relating to scaling up their businesses. The skills required by an entrepreneur were not necessarily the same as those needed by a larger company. The story of Death's Door Spirits in the US was a cautionary tale. The company had outstanding gins, but lack of business acumen meant that it went bankrupt in November 2018. It was reported that the original owners were good entrepreneurs, but lacked the business knowledge to cope with rapid growth, outrunning their profit margins and unable to pay their bills. They had grown too quickly and had no systems in place to cope with that growth. As a result, another distiller purchased the bankrupt company.

The onset of the pandemic

By far one of the darkest periods in the history of gin occurred in 2020. For over two decades, gin distilleries worldwide had been enjoying a dramatic renaissance, with sales booming.

The arrival of the Covid-19 pandemic with the onset of lockdowns closing bars, pubs, restaurants, entertainment venues and most shops marked a massive change in their fortunes. Overnight sales disappeared leaving many distilleries with no income, no customers, and facing the possibility of having to close. As Carmen O'Neal at London-based 58 Gin indicated, 'We suddenly had a business with no customers and no income.'

Survival came from an unlikely source. Demand for hand sanitiser skyrocketed, but there were insufficient supplies available. Gin companies quickly realised that they possessed supplies of a key ingredient: alcohol, in the form of ethanol. It was a massive undertaking at very short notice and involved a steep learning curve. News quickly spread throughout the industry of the existence of an approved WHO (World Health Organisation) sanitiser recipe. The instructions were easy to follow and the required ingredients were few in number: ethanol, hydrogen peroxide, glycerol and sterile distilled or boiled cold water, plus containers for mixing and distribution. There were some precautions that had to be taken, primarily with regard to potential fire risks – undiluted ethanol is highly flammable and needs to be stored well away from high temperatures or flames.

Within days, gin companies worldwide were transforming their production processes to create hand sanitiser. Big producers like William Grant & Sons provided vast quantities of low-priced ethanol for sanitiser production. Diageo donated 2 million litres of ethanol, allowing the creation of more than 8 million bottles of sanitiser for frontline healthcare staff across the UK, Italy, USA, Brazil, Kenya, India and Australia. In Venezuela, Canaïma Gin, part of DUSA (Destilerias Unidas), donated over 60,000 litres of alcohol to health authorities for the production of sanitisers. On a local basis, distilleries like the Isle of Man-based Fynoderee collaborated with local scientists and companies to produce 750 litres a week, enough to cater for the entire island.

Speed was essential. The Belgian-based Rubbens distillery secured the necessary permissions and extra ingredients and was able to set up production within two days. The first order from a hospital in Bruges arrived on the Monday, and was delivered the following day. Within days, the company had received cold calls seeking sanitiser from 20 hospitals and 300 pharmacies across Belgium and elsewhere in Europe. According to Hendrik Beck, owner of Rubbens, one of his drivers commented that it was almost like a party on arriving at a hospital in eastern Belgium. In Australia, the Sydney-based Archie Rose Distilling Company found its first production of 4,500 units of 500ml bottles sold out in less than an hour.

Emergency services and medical providers were quick to take advantage of the arrival of much needed sanitiser suppliers, for example, Durham health workers directly contacted Durham Distillery for infection control supplies.

Problems with HM Revenue & Customs

For most UK gin distillers, the biggest problem encountered during this period was from HM Revenue & Customs, which had to be contacted for a change of duty to allow alcohol to be turned into an alternative product. Its agreement was not always easy to obtain, and most distillers simply went ahead and manufactured and supplied sanitisers, forcing HMRC to back down due to the scale of public support.

A typical example was that of Old Bakery Gin in London. Faced with rejection by Revenue & Customs and told any appeal would take several weeks, they decided that it was more important to deal with the emergency requirements and adopted a rather innovative approach to the issue. The company was seeking to supply frontline services such as the MOD and British Army, and when Revenue & Customs rejected their request, the Old Bakery put out a YouTube video showing themselves making bootleg sanitiser.

Ian Puddick commented:

> The next thing I knew was that a big whisky manufacturer from Scotland was on the phone saying his daughter had shown him the video. He said they would provide the alcohol needed. I said we didn't have a licence. Their response was to say if there are any questions from Customs, tell them to speak to us – and began supplying us on an industrial scale.

Puddick personally hand-delivered a letter offering to supply sanitiser to the Cabinet Office at 8 p.m. on Sunday night, and within hours the Cabinet Office had asked them arrange distribution via the MOD/ British Army. From then on, the Old Bakery worked seven days a week making sanitiser which was collected by army trucks for distribution to army bases nationwide, as well as the MOD, Buckingham Palace and various other Royal households. Puddick added:

> I did stress that we were making it without a licence from Revenue & Customs, even though we were using the WHO formula. I was just told to pass any queries on – they would deal with it. Afterwards we received a handwritten letter from the colonel, based at the MOD, thanking us for making the sanitiser. All VAT and taxes were void.

Production problems

Added to the problem of ensuring a continuous supply of ethanol was the need to obtain packaging materials, setting up distribution methods and in some cases, having to re-tool stills in order to make the product to WHO standards at either 60% ABV for home use or 80% ABV for medical use.

Discovering that there was a difference in ABV requirements did cause some problems. Scotland-based company Brewdog donated its first batch to the local hospital free of charge, but the sanitiser was rejected because it did not meet the required medical standards. Although the sanitiser contained 68% alcohol, well above the 60% minimum recommended by the UK Health & Safety Executive, it did not meet clinical medical requirements. Brewdog swiftly collaborated with the medical authorities in the Grampian region to create a suitable sanitiser.

There were occasional mistakes and hitches to production that were quickly rectified. In Australia, the Victoria-based Apollo Bay Distillery found nine bottles of hand sanitiser were sold by accident as bottles of its SS Casino Gin. A product recall immediately went out for the bottles, which could be identified by the fact that they had no seal, and no shrink wrapping and consumers were warned that 'consumption of the product may have side effects including nausea, headaches, dizziness, bloating, vomiting, thirst and diarrhoea.'

By the summer of 2020, the Belgian Rubbens Distillery found itself producing almost twice as many gallons of hand sanitiser compared to gin each week, making it an important long-term, product line. As a result, a strange ritual has emerged which takes place several times each month. In order to prove that the alcohol-based sanitiser cannot be drunk for pleasure, a government official regularly visits the distillery to watch the distiller ceremonially pour ether into a vat of ethanol, thus rendering it undrinkable.

Packaging created a major problem as the high level of demand meant that there was a shortfall in the number of available containers. Distillers found themselves having to spend hours trying to source supplies. At the Caithness-based Dunnett Distillery, they chose recyclable bottles, and asked users to bring back the empties and place them in labelled boxes in the greenhouse. Dunnett staff cleaned and refilled the bottles before putting them back in the box for collection by local NHS practices, care homes and community groups.

Scale of involvement

There are no accurate figures as to the sheer number of gin distilleries or the quantities involved throughout the emergent phase of the pandemic. One estimate from the Scottish Gin Society quoted 439 European distillers who were believed to be participating in the hand sanitiser production, of which there were forty-seven in Scotland, four in Wales, twenty-three in England, three in Northern Ireland, and six in Ireland. Anecdotal evidence suggests that many others were involved on a smaller scale or more ad hoc basis.

What is certain is that from March 2020 onwards, millions of litres were produced within a short time. Almost all of this production was distributed within the community rather than being sold commercially. Looking back at those hectic months, producers believed they could have done more if only more containers had been available, and advice from Revenue & Customs had been less confusing.

For many gin makers, producing sanitiser was the only thing that kept them from going out of business, as most of the companies trade on slim margins and have no cash reserves. Shaun Ward, from Ludlow Gin, expressed the attitude of many distillers to the unprecedented situation in which they found themselves: 'When I started my gin-making career, I never believed I would be asking myself moral questions as to whether I should be doing something for commercial gain or not. These are exceptional times, it's not the time to think profits.'

For some companies, hand sanitiser production became a long-term business option. Typical examples were Durham Gin and Salcombe Gin, who opted to produce handbag-sized fashionable sanitisers. Bullards of Norwich expanded its activities supplying local leisure business and organisations such as motor dealers and golf courses while seeking out more attractive packaging in a glass bottle for the home, which can be refilled using pouches. Bullards regard the provision of sanitisers as an essential item that everyone now needs in their homes and businesses.

There can be little doubt that the impact made by gin distillers to communities coping with the virus was extremely important. 2020 saw gin distillers worldwide responding to one of the most serious pandemics in human history by turning their skills to serving their communities with the creation of hand sanitisers.

Surviving the pandemic

Following the initial shock reaction to the arrival of a pandemic and all that it meant for society generally, distillers were faced with the question of how to cope and continue trading. The introduction of social distancing, of reduced numbers within pubs and restaurants, along with the continued closure of many clubs and entertainment venues created a uniquely challenging trading environment that had not been previously encountered.

Some companies focused on developing their online businesses in response to consumer demand. Instead of going out for a drink, people were ordering online and drinking at home. Online gin sales were reported to have outstripped other spirits. 6 o'clock Gin found that its online sales had 'gone through the roof', while Masons Gin increased online activity by about 400 per cent. The Craft Gin Club reported a 70 per cent increase in membership, taking its subscriber list to over 90,000. By the end of 2020, the Wine and Spirit Trade Association noted that over 10 million extra bottles of gin had been purchased for drinking at home as the result of lockdowns and having to cope with the restrictions around the limited opening of licensed premises.

It was not just gin that experienced such high sales. Demand for mixers grew equally quickly. Fever-Tree mixers reported a 24 per cent increase in sales during the first month of lockdown. Doug Walford of Afterthought Gin said:

> April and May 2020 was insane. We were working 19–20 hours a day. A lot of firms like Cartier were ordering sanitiser from us. We had to improve our ecommerce site to cope with demand and had so many new return customers because they loved our product. To make it even easier for people, we linked with Fever-Tree to sell tonic at the same time as the gin. We gave a tonic as a freebie with a bottle of gin. It made us stand out. When people were stuck at home and panicking, searching for sanitisers and saw we were doing gin as well, sales went up. People could not go to bars and pubs, they were living in a virtual society and as a result of the pandemic we were able to cope and adapt very quickly.

In Scotland, the Old Poison Distillery even developed a lockdown Quarantine Spa Kit containing a relaxing mix of Selkie London Dry or Selkie Gold Pink or Vesuvius Elder, plus Fever-Tree tonics, bath salts and an Edinburgh essence diffuser or candle.

Harrogate Tipple combined hand sanitiser manufacture with producing gin, as well as running a drive-in market within its distillery yard, combining their wares with other local businesses including a baker and cheese producer. This enabled people from Ripley and the surrounding villages to buy the food and drink needed, while observing social distancing guidelines and not even having to leave their car.

At Dunnet Bay Distillery in Scotland, the distillery shop was turned into a grocery stocked with produce ordered through the company's wholesalers. Vulnerable people could pre-order and have goods delivered within a 3-mile radius, or drive up for a click and collect system.

Otterbeck Distillery decided to work with a Covid legend – Captain Sir Tom Moore – to launch a gin with all proceeds going to The Captain Tom Foundation, supporting The Royal British Legion,

Mind and other charities. Captain Tom, 100-year-old Second World War veteran, had set out to walk 100 laps of his garden as a way of raising funds. The story of his efforts went viral worldwide, resulting over £40m being raised. The British Army provided a guard of honour for his final lap, and the queen gave him a knighthood.

One small gin company set out to bring a smile and provide some help and respite. Dorset-based Ali Redwood set up Delilah's Gin during lockdown, naming it in honour of her dachshund. Ali commented:

> Like many dogs during the pandemic, Delilah has been the perfect companion. Small businesses are the heartbeat of the UK economy. And with more uncertain times ahead, supporters of fledgling British firms could be the lynchpin in keeping them afloat. Delilah's mastery is in making people smile. We thought what better time to encapsulate her smooth and unique spirit within an artisanal small-batch gin and share it during these challenging times.

As businesses reopened, social distancing measures resulted in new trading problems. Tasting gin before buying had always been a popular retailing method within distillery stores, but the impact of Covid made this much harder to achieve safely for both staff and customers. York Gin created an innovative solution, by taking an example from the past. It updated the eighteenth-century Puss and Mew vending system. The company created a special wood and Perspex dispensing area. Images of cats were engraved into the Perspex, along with the provision of tubes extending from the staff area into the customer area. Customers choose the gin they wish to try, and a sample is poured down the appropriate cat tube into a disposable cup.

Emma Godiva of York Gin commented:

> We have a cat in our logo and we had been toying with the idea of creating a Puss 'n' Mew machine but had been struggling

to find a practical use for it. Customers love the revamped Puss 'n' Mew. They adore that we have been inspired by gin's murky and disreputable past to create a machine that makes tasting gin during the pandemic safe and enjoyable.

Going forward

The effects of the pandemic affected gin distillers in many unexpected ways – and in some cases, gin even provided a change of occupation. Essex-based entrepreneur Mel Sims operated a play centre business that closed due to lockdown and social distancing rules. Looking around for a way to create an income, she realised she had been drinking a lot more gin and tonics to get through the lockdown and came up with the idea of producing a range of healthy gins. Mel set up Mooze Booze alternative gin, which as well as being sugar free, vegan-friendly and low alcohol, utilises six different botanical flavours. She began selling it directly to the public and planning a mobile gin bar.

Despite the initial worries at the onset of the pandemic, gin distillers survived. Being small, flexible and versatile provided to be a saviour. Distillers were faced with making quick decisions and seizing every opportunity that arose.

An unexpected result of the various lockdowns experienced throughout 2020 and 2021 was that distillery numbers continued to expand. Entrepreneurs took advantage of the quieter period and the opportunity to think and plan by setting up businesses. In the UK, figures released by HMRC indicated that over 100 new UK distilleries were registered for the first time during that tumultuous year.

Yet as 2021 dawned, it was clear that further challenges faced the gin industry. Sales were still struggling due to the closure of the vast array of social venues that traditionally accounted for the majority of gin sales. The loss of the wholesale gin sector was massive, and continual lockdowns and social distancing made it harder for licensed premises to cope. Many such venues closed permanently in 2020.

Consultants CGA Strategy reported a net decline of around 6,000 licensed premises during 2020. One in five hospitality businesses were indicating that they did not have the cash to continue trading after February 2021. The resultant figures bore this out: 2,713 licensed premises in Britain closed during January and February of that year.

Local provenance

Regaining customer confidence in visiting licensed social venues became a challenge for licensed premises as well as distillers. The rise in the number of community pubs owned by the local community provided opportunities for regional brands. Local provenance is becoming one of the key trends in gin distilling. Many small distillers hold special workshops taking people out into the locality to pick their own botanicals in order to make a bespoke gin, as well as seeking out local produce for their own gin brands. Nottingham-based Weavers, for example, forage acorns from local forests including Sherwood for production of their Castle Gate Gin. Another Nottingham-based distillers, Redsmith, have taken an iconic local product, the Bramley Apple, to create a unique gin. Wayne Asher of Redsmith said:

> I've always been fascinated by gin history and I came across an old recipe for apple gin, a compounded product with the apple added post distillation. There doesn't seem to have been an apple gin since the 1940s. The birthplace of the Bramley apple is nearby and it is an apple known throughout the world. The Bramley apples we use are collected from descendants of the original tree.

Worcester-based Hussingtree Gin focuses on the importance of local provenance for its products. The name is derived from a local village, with fruit and botanicals sourced within the immediate region. The only person growing juneberries in the UK lives in Worcestershire, which is why they chose juneberries for their first gin. It became a conversation piece as customers immediately started asking about these unusual fruits.

A visit to the Pershore Plum Festival provided the inspiration for the company's Plum Gin, and although Bumbleberries is an American term, it actually refers to a type of fruit available only in autumn. Hussingtree opted to use typical wild fruits including blackberry, bilberry and sloe.

Slingsby Gin is another company stressing the importance of local provenance. Its Original Yorkshire Rhubarb Gin campaign ran on Sky TV showcasing rhubarb from the long-established Yorkshire Triangle of producers alongside Slingsby's home town of Harrogate.

Just as in other food and drink sectors, the concept of fair trading has also entered the gin industry. Leading the fair trading activities is a specialist distiller, Fair Spirits. Paul Bungener of Fair says:

> Fair as a concept has grown tremendously, it is easy to understand. People are seeking provenance and want to know where items come from. All aspects of our brand have to be sustainable. Not just the ingredients, we had to look at the bottles and liquids and every aspect of the production including labelling and caps. We have even found a way to ensure a plastic-free seal.

Sustainability & climate change

Sustainability and climate change have become the watchwords for the twenty-first century, creating issues set to form another chapter in the history of gin.

One of the biggest issues may well come from one of its key ingredients: juniper. Scientists have raised concerns over the future of juniper trees. An invasive pathogen, Phytophthora austrocedri, has begun attacking juniper trees in Scotland – a country responsible for approximately 70 per cent of the juniper in the UK. Thousands of trees could be lost. Professor Gurr from the University of Exeter commented: 'At a time of heightened awareness of the impact of epidemics on human health, we must also remember that disease has a huge impact upon plant health. Disease devastates not only human life, but also crops and the very calories we need to sustain us.'

Although distillers have access to other sources of juniper, particularly in Italy and Macedonia, the potential decrease in Scottish juniper berries will be a major blow to the industry. Crossbill Distillery emphasised the extent of the damage to a native tree that should be able to flourish. 'Its population is declining due to years of mismanagement and Phytophthora austrocedrae, a pathogen that infects and kills our juniper trees.'

Andrew Heald, of Fishers Gin, comments: 'Sustainability is a focus and this only increases our reliance on imports. I'm trying to grow my own here in Suffolk, but I certainly can't rely on them.' Ultimately, the question is whether the pathogen will attack juniper trees elsewhere, as the results could be catastrophic for the industry. Paul Bungener of Fair has even suggested that the sheer size of the industry, with ever-increasing numbers of distillers appearing throughout the world, could mean that 'we risk running out of juniper eventually. I believe it will have an impact in about ten to fifteen years.'

Operating methods

Even the containers that hold the gin are coming under scrutiny. Glass bottles are expensive to produce, and transportation costs can be high. Alternative options are increasingly being sought as a way of reducing carbon footprints. Several companies such as Bullards and Dunnet Bay have begun to offer refillable packs or eco pouches that reduce volume, packaging and transported weight. Silent Pool Distillers took the sustainability concept even further by launching the world's first gin in a paperboard bottle. The company's Green

Man Woodland Gin uses a bottle produced by Frugalpac which is five times lighter than glass bottles, uses 77 per cent less plastic and has a carbon footprint six times lower than glass or PET plastic bottles. The paperboard layer is made from 94 per cent paper and the interior pouch can be easily separated, making it 100 per cent recyclable. As Sophie Best, General Manager at Silent Pool Distillers indicates, 'We're located in the UK's most wooded county and surrounded by amazing ancient woodland. This inspired us to create a spirit that truly captures the environment, and to package that liquid in a way that significantly reduces the environmental impact.'

Changes in operating procedures have begun to appear. Gin distilling is traditionally a heavy user of water and energy. In order to become more sustainable and be able to cope with the demands of climate change, it means that changes are inevitable. North Yorkshire's Cooper King Distillery is one of a handful of UK distilleries running on 100 per cent green energy, while using vacuum stills to reduce energy and save water. A closed loop system enables coolant water to be constantly reused, thus saving 26 tonnes of water annually. As an extra benefit, its waste botanicals are sent to a local bakery to be turned into bread and pastry glazes. Other methods being adopted by distillers include sourcing surplus produce rejected by supermarkets, avoiding plastic materials, using green energy resources like solar panels, turning waste into biofuels and utilising heat generated from waste to pre-heat the next distillation.

A more unusual option has been adopted by Arbikie, Scotland's field to bottle distillery, which has turned to peas for its main product. Described as the world's first climate positive gin (avoiding more carbon dioxide emissions than it creates) the Nàdar Gin is distilled from peas rather than cereals due to the fact that peas require no synthetic nitrogen fertilisers to be added to the soil, instead providing a natural benefit. As a result there is no negative environmental impact on either soil or waterways.

Gin and animal conservation

Animal conservation has also attracted attention from distillers. African elephants are a highly endangered species, threatened not only by predators and ivory poachers but also by climate change, and human demand for living space. Conserving these creatures is important, and has led to the creation of gins designed to help attract attention while providing valuable additional funds.

Elephant dung is not an ingredient one would normally associate with gin, but that is exactly what Indlovu uses. Named after the Zulu word for elephant, Indlovu describes itself as 'an innovative premium gin for the adventurous spirit'. Drinkers discover the 'true taste of Africa in every glass', with every batch possessing distinct local provenance. The dung comes from elephants in the Botlierskop Game Reserve and depending on the locale where and when the dung is collected, the botanicals present vary creating infusions of different flavours, thus resulting in gin vintages, just like wine. Each bottle of Indlovu Gin contains a lot number combining the date of dung collection with the exact geographical co-ordinates. The idea for the gin resulted from a visit to a game reserve and the discovery that elephants are very particular in their browsing, yet actually digest very little of the plant material they eat. The dung is collected, washed and dried, allowing the botanicals to be extracted. These include a range of native flowers, bark, leaves, nuts, and fruits – whatever the elephant has chosen to eat. Following maceration, sterilisation and re-drying, the ingredients are combined using multiple flavouring runs to create the final product. Fifteen per cent of the profits go back into wildlife conservation via the African Foundation. Unconfirmed reports suggest that the distillery's consultant came up with words 'if you're going to make a gin from shit, you can't make a shit gin.'

For those interested in helping elephant conservation who can't stomach the idea of drinking something with its origins in dung, Elephant Gin takes a slightly different path. Tessa Gerlach, co-owner of the brand explains:

I am fascinated by elephants and wanted to help in their conservation. My husband's passion was gin, so we had the idea of creating an Elephant Gin. Gin has always been strong in South Africa and Kenya, with its tradition of sundown gin and tonics. We focused on native African botanicals such as Buchu, Lions Tail and Dragons Claw.

One of the most striking aspects of the Elephant Gin is the packaging, deliberately designed to stand out and attract attention both to the product and elephant conservation. The bottle is reminiscent of a flask used by hunters on safari, while the map used on the label was inspired by the history of botanists who gathered plants in South Africa. The linen-covered gift boxes are adorned on the interior with intricate maps created by a calligrapher, along with links to named elephants. Even tissue paper wrapping contains maps and elephant images. Packaging material involves locally made, sustainable products.

A different elephant is portrayed in each box, and people can go on to the company's website to find out more about specific elephants. It is a popular concept, as the company have had queries about elephants when it has not uploaded information sufficiently quickly. Typical stories included that of Ulysses, a 39-year-old bull living at the Amboseli National Park, and the more tragic story of Mountain Bull, who was slain by poachers for his tusks.

Fifteen per cent of the price of each bottle of gin is donated to elephant charities and foundations with which they work. By 2020 over 700,000 euros had been donated; as a result providing funds for an education centre promoting conservation, salaries for forty-five anti-poaching rangers and supporting twenty-three elephant orphans living in an elephant sanctuary.

Although no one knows the challenges yet to be faced by the gin industry, the past 400 years have shown it to be resilient and able to overcome obstacles. Long may its success continue!

Resources

Barnett, Richard, *The Book of Gin: A Spirited history from Alchemists' Stills and Colonial Outposts to Gin Palaces, Bathtub Gin and Artisanal Cocktails*, Grove Press 2011

Blumenthal, Heston, *Heston's Fantastical Feasts*, Bloomsbury 2010

Bradstreet, Dudley, *The Life and Uncommon Adventures of Captain Dudley Bradstreet*, 1755

Carver, Stephen, *The 19th Century Underworld Crime Controversy and Corruption*, Pen & Sword Publishing 2018

Dillon, Patrick Justin, *Gin: The Much Lamented Death of Madam Geneva – the Eighteenth-Century Gin Craze*, Charles & Company 2004

George, M. Dorothy, *London Life in the Eighteenth Century*, Penguin Books 1925

Hicks, Dr Rob, *Old-Fashioned Remedies from Arsenic to Gin*, Pen & Sword Publishing 2009

Hipper, Kenneth, *Smugglers: All Centuries of Norfolk Smuggling*, Larks Press 2001

Platt, Richard, *Smuggling in the British Isles*, The History Press 2011

Rowley, Matthew, *Lost Recipes of Prohibition: Notes from a Bootlegger's Manual*, Countryman Press 2015

Stephenson, Tristan, *The Curious Bartender's Gin Palace*, Ryland Peters & Small 2016

Williams, Olivia, *Gin Glorious Gin: How Mother's Ruin Became the Spirit of London*, Headline 2014

Wilson, Bee, *Swindled: From Poison Sweets to Counterfeit Coffee – The Dark History of the Food Cheats*, John Murray 2008

Wilson, Ben, *Decency & Disorder The Age of Cant 1789–1837*, Faber & Faber 2007

Index